RELATING TO OTHERS IN LOVE

A Study of Romans 12-16

BIBLE STUDY GUIDE

From the Bible-teaching ministry of

Charles R. Swindoll

INSIGHT FOR LIVING

Chuck graduated in 1963 from Dallas Theological Seminary, where he now serves as the school's fourth president, helping to prepare a new generation of men and women for the ministry. Chuck has served in pastorates in three states: Massachusetts, Texas, and California, including almost twenty-three years at the First Evangelical Free Church in Fullerton, California. He is currently senior pastor of Stonebriar Community Church in Frisco, Texas, north of Dallas. His sermon messages have been aired over radio since 1979 as the *Insight for Living* broadcast. A best-selling author, Chuck has written numerous books and booklets on many subjects.

Based on the outlines and transcripts of Chuck's sermons, the study guide text is co-authored by Jason Shepherd, a graduate of the Texas A&M University and Dallas Theological Seminary. He also wrote the Living Insights.

Editor in Chief:	**Text Designer:**
Cynthia Swindoll	Gary Lett
Senior Writer:	**Graphic System Administrator:**
Jason Shepherd	Bob Haskins
Senior Editor and Assistant Writer:	**Publishing System Specialist:**
Wendy Peterson	Alex Pasieka
Copy Editors:	**Director, Communications Division:**
Karla Lenderink	John Norton
Marco Salazar	**Project Coordinator:**
Glenda Schlahta	Shannon Scharkey

Unless otherwise identified, all Scripture references are from the New American Standard Bible, updated edition, copyright © The Lockman Foundation 1960, 1962, 1963, 1968, 1971, 1972, 1973, 1975, 1977, 1995. Used by permission. Scripture taken from the Holy Bible, New International Version © 1973, 1978, 1984 International Bible Society, used by permission of Zondervan Bible Publishers [NIV]. Other versions cited are the *New Testament in Modern English* (PHILLIPS), the *New King James Version* (NKJV), and the *New English Bible* (NEB).

Some material in chapters 3, 5, 6, 11, 13, 16 is from *Romans: God's Good News to the World* by John R. W. Stott, © 1994 by John Stott. Used by permission of InterVarsity Press, P. O. Box 1400, Downers Grove, IL 60515.

Life Application Bible Commentary: *Romans*, copyright 1992 by the Livingstone Corporation. Used by permission of Tyndale House Publishers. All rights reserved.

An effort has been made to locate sources and obtain permission where necessary for the quotations used in this book. In the event of any unintentional omission, a modification will gladly be incorporated in future printings.

ISBN 1-57972-260-1
Study Guide Cover Design: Eric Chimenti
Cover Photograph: © The Stock Market/Ted Horowitz, 1999
Printed in the United States of America

CONTENTS

INTRODUCTION

The value of Romans is legendary. Down through the centuries Christians have turned to this book perhaps more often than any other in the Bible. It gives our faith backbone. It strengthens our confidence in our God. It clarifies our understanding of the salvation we have received. It lifts our sights above the petty irritations of life on earth and reminds us of our sure hope in the Lord Jesus Christ.

But that only covers the first eleven chapters! When we arrive at the twelfth chapter—one of the greatest in Scripture—we begin to walk on new terrain. The focus shifts to relationships, with those inside the family of God as well as those outside. Instead of an emphasis on doctrine and hope, the theme changes to authentic love for one another.

I am pleased to continue traveling with you along the Romans' road. This section, Romans 12–16, is exceedingly practical—my kind of truth! So let's be open and ready to hear what God's Spirit has to say about relating to others in love.

Chuck Swindoll

Chuck Swindoll

PUTTING TRUTH
INTO ACTION

Knowledge apart from application falls short of God's desire for His children. He wants us to apply what we learn so that we will change and grow. This study guide was prepared with these goals in mind. As you go through the following pages, we hope your desire to discover biblical truth will grow as your understanding of God's Word increases and that you will be encouraged to apply what you've learned.

To assist you in your study, we've included a section called ☼☼ **Living Insights** at the end of each lesson. These exercises will challenge you to study further and to think of specific ways to put your discoveries into action.

There are many ways to use this guide—in personal devotions, group studies, discussions with friends and family, and Sunday school classes. And, of course, it's an ideal study aid when you're listening to its corresponding *Insight for Living* radio series.

To benefit most from this study guide, we would encourage you to consider it a spiritual journal. That's why we've included space in the **Living Insights** for recording your thoughts and discoveries. We hope you'll return to those sections often for review and encouragement as you continue to grow in your walk with Christ.

Jason Shepherd

Jason Shepherd
Coauthor of Text
Author of Living Insights

RELATING TO OTHERS IN LOVE

A Study of Romans 12-16

KEY WORDS AND CONCEPTS IN ROMANS

We offer this list of theological terms to help you more fully understand and apply the rich truths found in Paul's letter to the Romans. We suggest you read through the list as you begin your study, then use it as a reference guide while working your way through Romans.

Condemnation: God's judicial pronouncement of sinful humanity's guilt before Him. It is a declaration of our depravity and the punishment we deserve for it. Condemnation is the opposite of justification, which is God's pronouncement of our righteousness in Christ. Once we place our trust in Christ, we are no longer under condemnation (Rom. 8:1). Rather, we are justified—pronounced righteous by God because we are clothed in the righteousness of His Son (Rom. 3:21–26; 5:1–2, 9).

Faith: The unqualified acceptance of and dependence on the completed work of Jesus Christ to secure God's mercy toward believers. It is the instrumental cause of our salvation, the means by which we are linked to Christ and allowed to receive God's gracious gift of justification. True faith includes *knowledge* that there is a holy God who gave His Son to reconcile sinners to Himself; *assent*, which means being intellectually convinced of the truth of that knowledge; and *volition*, being so convinced of the truth that we place our trust in Christ (Rom. 1:17; 3:22, 30; Heb. 11:1).

Flesh: Used in a theological sense, *flesh* doesn't refer to our physical body. Rather, it refers to our orientation and identity before God saved us—we were unbelievers, controlled and enslaved by sin, rejecters of God, people who preferred sin over righteousness. The flesh still tries to control us, but it no longer has any claim on us, since as Christians we now belong to Christ and walk in His Spirit (see Rom. 7:5, 14, 18, 25; 8:9).

Foreknowledge: In its most general sense, *foreknowledge* is God's knowing all things before they come to pass. It is more, though,

xiii

than God's simply having information ahead of time. God knows what will come to pass because He determines what will come to pass (see *predestination*). When specifically applied to salvation, foreknowledge is God's knowing us before we knew Him, before He even created us. When the Bible speaks of God's knowing people, it means He has made them the objects of His special love. Foreknowledge, then, is a word of determined choosing. God loved believers and chose them to be His own long before they put their trust in Him. To say that God foreknew us is to say He "foreloved" us (Acts 2:23; Rom. 8:29; 1 Pet. 1:1–2).

Glorification: The consummation of salvation. It occurs, in one sense, when we die and enter the presence of the Lord. At that point we will be completely free from the presence of sin. Glorification, however, occurs at its fullest when all who have died in Christ—as well as believers who are alive at Christ's return—will receive perfect, incorruptible bodies that will last for eternity. The process of sanctification will then be complete. We will be with Jesus and like Jesus—free from the presence of sin and perfect in body and soul (Rom. 8:23, 30; 1 Cor. 15:50–54; 1 John 3:2).

Gospel: The gospel, in a phrase, is "the joyous proclamation of God's redemptive activity in Christ Jesus on behalf of man enslaved by sin."[1] When we embrace the gospel by faith, we believe that Jesus lived and died for us, paying the penalty for our sins and providing us forgiveness; and that He was raised victoriously and bodily from the grave and lives for us today. All of this is motivated and accomplished by God's grace. This good news of salvation in Christ appears in the Old Testament in the form of promises, prophecies, and foreshadowing images (e.g., the promise of a redeemer in Genesis 3:15, the Passover lamb in Exodus 12, the prophecy of Christ's crucifixion in Isaiah 53, and the sacrificial system detailed in Leviticus). In the New Testament, the bright truth of the gospel bursts forth in all its glory. The four Gospels present the words and works of Christ. Acts chronicles the spread of the gospel in the known world, and the epistles explain the gospel and all its implications for

---

1. Robert H. Mounce, "Gospel," in *Evangelical Dictionary of Theology*, ed. Walter A. Elwell (Grand Rapids, Mich.: Baker Books, 1984), p. 472.

living the Christian life. And Revelation promises the consummation of our salvation, as Christ returns to claim His church. Not surprisingly, Paul used the word *gospel* some sixty times in his epistles. The message of salvation in Christ and all that means for living was the core of his message and mission (Rom. 1:15–17; 1 Cor. 15:1–4; Gal. 1:6–9; Phil. 1:12).

Grace: Unmerited favor freely granted to believers in Christ. When we say we're saved by grace, we mean that salvation comes to us, not by our ability to earn God's favor or live up to His standards, but by His free gift to us. Although salvation is a free gift, it cost God a great deal—the incarnation and death of His Son. One writer defined grace with the acrostic God's Riches At Christ's Expense.[2] Instead of receiving the judgment we deserve for our sin, we will spend an eternity in the blessed presence of our Lord. All because of grace (Rom. 5:15–17, 21; 6:14; Eph. 2:4–8; Titus 3:4–7).

Justification: God's declaration or pronouncement that sinners, upon believing in Christ, are righteous because of Christ—even though still in a sinning state (Rom. 3:23–24; Gal. 3:11). As such, we are assured of God's blessings toward us and need no longer fear His wrath or condemnation. Justification is an instantaneous act of God that begins the Christian life. Once justified (declared righteous), the Christian begins the process of sanctification (growing in Christ).

Law: God's moral demands on His created human beings. The Law reflects God's holy character and His purposes for the people He created. His Law is summarized in the Ten Commandments (Exod. 20:1–17) and more fully explained by Jesus in the Gospels (Matt. 5:21–22, 27–28) and by Paul and other New Testament writers. God's Law in the Old Testament included civil laws for the theocratic nation of Israel and ceremonial laws (sacrifices, kosher diet, etc.) that taught the need for moral purity. God still demands moral perfection from His human creatures. But unregenerate sinners cannot keep God's Law. They hate it, in fact. The Law exposes our sinfulness and our need for God's grace (Rom. 7:7). And that is the Law's main

---

2. As quoted by Ray C. Stedman in *Birth of the Body* (Santa Ana, Calif.: Vision House Publishers, 1974), p. 98.

purpose. It cannot make us righteous, but it drives us to Christ, who kept the Law perfectly and who clothes us with His own righteousness (Gal. 3:23–29). Once saved, Christians no longer hate the Law. They agree with God that His moral demands are good, and they strive to obey Him—not to earn salvation, but out of gratitude for salvation (Ps. 19:7–11; 119:35; Rom. 8:3–4; 12:1).

Predestination: In its wider sense, the word refers to God's predetermining whatever comes to pass—His working "all things after the counsel of His will" (Eph. 1:11b). In its narrower sense, which specifically relates to salvation, predestination refers to God's selecting out of sinful humanity a multitude of people He would save through Christ (Rom. 8:29; Eph. 1:4–6; see also Jer. 1:5). This narrower sense of predestination is also referred to as election. Election is closely related to foreknowledge but differs from it in that foreknowledge tells us God loved us in eternity past, whereas election tells us what that love accomplished—our salvation.

Propitiation: The satisfaction of God's wrath against sin through the sacrifice of His Son on the cross (Rom. 3:25–26). God is holy; humanity is sinful. Because God cannot excuse or condone sin, He must punish it. In His grace, He sent Jesus Christ to suffer His wrath in our place. Thus, the Cross upholds God's character as both a righteous Judge and a merciful Savior—the just One and the One who justifies (Rom. 3:26).

Righteousness: When applied to God, the word refers to His good, perfect, and holy nature and His ability to do only what is right. God cannot sin. He cannot condone sin. He cannot be unjust. And He cannot err. He always and in every way acts in accord with His perfect moral nature. When applied to humans, righteousness is what God demands of us in terms of how we live. He requires that we live in perfect obedience to His moral law— that we conform to it inwardly as well as outwardly. Since no one is able to do this (Paul says in Romans 3:10 that "there is none righteous, not even one"), someone must earn righteousness for us. That's what Jesus did. He lived a perfectly obedient life under the Law. His every thought, motive, action, and word was pleasing to the Father. Then He died on the cross to take the punishment for our unrighteousness. When we put our trust in Jesus, His righteousness is imputed to us—that is, God counts us as righteous, even though we still sin . . . because Christ has given His righteousness to us. Believers grow in righteousness in this life but will never be perfectly righteous until heaven.

Salvation: God's delivering us from the penalty, power, and presence of sin. Immediately upon believing in Jesus, we are delivered from the penalty of sin (eternal damnation) and the power of sin (its mastery over our lives). When we finally see the Lord face-to-face, we will be free from the presence of sin. Salvation includes not only our souls but our bodies as well, which will be resurrected on the last day.

Sanctification: When we put our trust in Christ, we were made righteous *positionally*; God declared us righteous (justified us) because of the life and death of His Son. But justification also marks the beginning of sanctification —the process of our becoming righteous *practically*, being set apart to God by the Spirit to grow out of sin and more fully into Christ. We will never be perfectly sanctified until heaven, but we will move toward perfection. We will change. We will, by the power of the Holy Spirit, conform more and more to the will of God and live lives that are pleasing to Him (Rom. 6:19; 1 Thess. 4:3–7; 5:23). Sin will always be present with us in this life, but its influence over us will be lessened over time in the process of sanctification.

Sin: Sin is both a condition and an expression. We are sinful by nature, born corrupt (Ps. 51:5; Rom. 3:10–11; Eph. 2:1). And that condition naturally produces thoughts and actions that violate God's Law (Gal. 5:19–21). Salvation in Christ is the only way to escape God's wrath toward sin and enter a life in which sin no longer controls us. Christians have the assurance that we will be free once and for all from the presence of sin when we step out of this life and into the next.

Works: We can view human works in two ways. One is to see them as deeds performed to earn God's favor so that He will repay us with salvation. The Bible is very clear that such a system of salvation is futile, since none of us can live righteously enough to keep God's Law (Rom. 3:9–18, 20; Gal. 3:10). That is why we must trust in Christ, whose works were perfect under the Law (Rom. 3:21–26; 5:6–11; 2 Cor. 5:21; Heb. 4:15). The Christian, however, has a second way to view works: good works grow out of our new life in Christ (Rom. 6:1–2, 11–13; 8:29; Gal. 5:22–24; Eph. 2:8–10; James 2:14–26; 1 John 3:16–19; 4:19–21). Indwelled by God's Spirit and in gratitude for what Christ has done for us, Christians do deeds that are pleasing to Him. When we sin, however, we need to remember that our salvation is still secure and that we have forgiveness, thanks to the perfect lawkeeping and sacrificial death of Jesus.

ROMANS

THE GOSPEL . . .

	. . . Saving the Sinner		. . . Concerning Israel	. . . Concerning Christian Conduct
	Depravity of humanity / Grace of God / Justification by faith / Sanctification through the Spirit / Security of the saint		Divine sovereignty and human will / Past, present, and future of the nation	Social / Civil / Personal
	CHAPTERS 1:18–8:39		*CHAPTERS 9–11*	*CHAPTERS 12:1–15:13*
Emphasis	Doctrinal		National	Practical
Response	Faith		Hope	Love
Doctrine of God	Wrath	Righteousness	Glory	Grace
Doctrine of Humanity	Fallen	Dead	Saved / Struggling	Freed
Doctrine of Sin	Exposed	Conquered	Explained	Forgiven
Scope	Dead in sin	Dead to sin	Peace with God	Love for others
Main Theme	God's righteousness is given to those who put their faith in Jesus Christ.			
Key Verses	1:16–17			

Chapter 1

HOW FAITH FUNCTIONS

Romans 12:1–8

Think of the book of Romans as a crossword puzzle. For eleven chapters, the apostle Paul has been filling in a lot of doctrinal blanks for us:

DOWN
1. Humanity's depraved state.
2. God's unmerited favor.
3. Our means for availing ourselves of God's unmerited favor.
4. The part of ourselves that tries to sidetrack our faith.
5. God declaring us righteous while we're still in a sinning state.
6. The process of the Holy Spirit making us righteous.
7. God's predetermining and electing activity.
8. We can never be separated from Christ's _____.

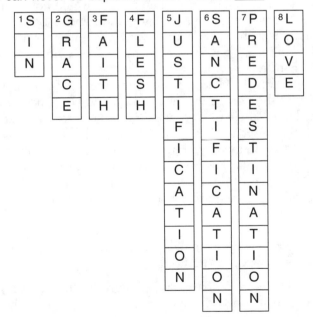

Yes, Paul has been filling in a lot of blanks for us, but there's still something missing in our puzzle. All these concepts that Paul has taught us about so far only fill the vertical spaces. That is, Paul has dealt almost exclusively with the vertical relationship between God and us. What about the words that go across, the horizontal aspects of the Christian faith?

How Christians relate horizontally—with one another—will be Paul's focus in Romans 12–16. He shifts his attention to the practical side of faith: the ways believers interact with each other and the world, how our knowledge becomes practice—how we relate to others in love.

In chapter 12, then, Paul begins to balance the vertical with the horizontal, the doctrinal with the relational. He focuses on the practical outworking of the faith by showing his readers how to see people with God's eyes, how to love them with His heart, how to speak to them with His lips, and how to serve them with His hands and feet. Before this kind of service can take place, however, Christians first must prepare their hearts and minds through a process we'll call "looking within."

Looking Within

Paul knew that relating to others in love would not come automatically. The world system, our own flesh, and Satan himself all work to entice us into loving only ourselves, into ignoring God in a lifestyle that seeks only our own pleasure. The Christian life takes effort. It's hard to resist our selfish urges.

The only way, in fact, to resist those urges is to have a strong foundation in the Lord, a life deeply rooted in Him and committed to serving Him. People who possess this kind of faith usually practice three habits: consecrating their lives to the Lord, allowing themselves to be transformed by Him, and evaluating their abilities and attitudes on a regular basis. Combined, these habits make up the process of looking within, a concept which can help us tie together the life-changing principles contained in Romans 12:1–3.

Consecration

Paul begins his discussion by urging the Roman believers to consecrate their lives to the Lord.

> Therefore I urge you, brethren, by the mercies
> of God, to present your bodies a living and holy

sacrifice, acceptable to God, which is your spiritual service of worship. (v. 1)

Paul's word choice here is interesting. He doesn't merely suggest or wish; he *urges*. In other words, consecration is more than a good idea—it's something that Paul knows is essential to the Christian life.

What exactly does *consecration* mean? Simply put, it means "set apart or reserved for God." In the way a table at a restaurant is saved for a specific guest or a seat on a plane is set aside for a particular traveler, so Christians set themselves apart for God. We continually put ourselves at His disposal—for His use, His glory, His will, His pleasure—for Him only.

Paul employs a strong image in the verse to communicate the nature of this consecrated life. He calls it "a living sacrifice." Most of us associate sacrifice with death—such as an animal chosen and killed for the specific purpose of being burned on an altar. Paul, however, describes Christians as *living* sacrifices. We're dead in the sense that we no longer live for ourselves, but we're alive in that we now live for God. We daily lay aside our own desires to follow Him.[1] The problem with living sacrifices, though, is that they often crawl off the altar!

So don't become discouraged if you find yourself off the altar. Consecration is a process, one that takes a daily—if not hourly—commitment to live for God. In this process, we give our lives over to the Lord and learn more and more how to love others with His love.

Transformation

In addition to consecration, looking within also involves transformation.

And do not be conformed to this world, but be transformed by the renewing of your mind, so that you may prove what the will of God is, that which is good and acceptable and perfect. (v. 2)

Many of us struggle to become *transformed* for God because we're being *conformed* to the world. What a tragedy! Nothing could be more unnatural for a believer in Christ than to become a disciple of the world.

---

1. See Bruce B. Barton, David R. Veerman, and Neil Wilson, *Romans*, The Life Application Bible Commentary Series (Wheaton, Ill.: Tyndale House Publishers, 1992), p. 230. Used by permission.

The very nature of the words in this verse emphasizes Paul's point here. We could define the word *conform*, in fact, as "an outward expression of something that doesn't come from within." When we wrap ourselves around the things that characterize the world system—its goals of fortune, fame, power, and pleasure—we are conforming to forces outside our reborn nature (see 2 Cor. 5:17).

To be *transformed*, however, means "to assume an outward expression of an inner reality." We take on a new shape because of a force from within. Pressed cookies are made by being conformed; butterflies are made by being transformed.[2] J. B. Phillips highlights this contrast:

> Don't let the world around you squeeze you into its own mold, but let God re-make you so that your whole attitude of mind is changed. (v. 2a PHILLIPS)

The natural outworking of our vertical consecration to God is having our "whole attitude of mind" changed in our horizontal relationships as well. The apostle John tells us: "The one who loves God should love his brother also" (1 John 4:21). One of the greatest marks of spiritual maturity is loving others, and this should be one of the most natural acts a Christian performs. When we allow God to make our minds and hearts new, then sharing with and ministering to others becomes our joy. And we show to all the world just how good and acceptable and perfect—how pure and beautiful—God's will is.

Evaluation

One final preparation of the heart and mind needs to be made before the hands and feet are engaged in loving service:

> For through the grace given to me I say to everyone among you not to think more highly of himself than he ought to think; but to think so as to have sound judgment, as God has allotted to each a measure of faith. (Rom. 12:3)

Evaluation. Paul wants each of us to have a proper appraisal of

---

2. "The Greek verb translated 'transformed' (*metamorphousthe*) is seen in the English word 'metamorphosis,' a total change from the inside out (cf. 2 Cor. 3:18)." John A. Witmer, "Romans," in *The Bible Knowledge Commentary*, New Testament edition, ed. John F. Walvoord and Roy B. Zuck (Colorado Springs, Colo.: Chariot Victor Publishing, 1983), p. 487.

ourselves and to stop and take stock of our attitudes. Namely, he wants us to keep a check on our pride.

Now let's add a second word to this principle: *honest* evaluation. Let's face it, most of us lack an honest assessment of ourselves. Some of us think more highly of ourselves than we ought, others think too lowly. Both mind-sets cause destruction. We're neither indispensable nor worthless, and we certainly can't do everything. God has "allotted," or gifted, each of us to do a few things well; and with true humility—which is knowing ourselves, accepting who we are, and being satisfied with our place in God's program—we can do them to His glory. As Commentators Bruce B. Barton, David R. Veerman, and Neil Wilson sum up:

> God has given each believer a *measure of faith* with which to serve him. This expression refers to the spiritual capacity and/or power given to each person to carry out his or her function in the church. . . . Whatever we have in the way of natural abilities or spiritual gifts—all should be used with humility for building up the body of Christ. If we are proud, we cannot exercise our faith and gifts to benefit others. And if we consider ourselves worthless, we also withhold what God intended to deliver to others through us.[3]

The process of looking within, then, involves three phases. First, we consecrate our lives to God. Second, we allow Him to transform us. And finally, we evaluate ourselves accurately to know how we can best serve others. And our service to others is Paul's next topic.

Serving Others

Paul now turns to the subject of service and gifts in the church.

In Principle

He first lays out the complementary relationship between two ideals that often seem at odds with each other: unity and diversity.

> For just as we have many members in one body and all the members do not have the same function, so we, who are many, are one body in Christ, and individually members one of another. (vv. 4–5)

3. Barton, Veerman, and Wilson, *Romans*, p. 233.

Can diversity and unity exist simultaneously? According to Paul, they not only *can*, but they *must!* To explain this complex concept, he invokes the image of a human body. On one hand, the body has many parts: feet, hands, legs, arms, torso, and a head. On the other hand, it has a singular purpose. All the different parts work together to achieve a common goal.

So it is with the body of Christ. Diversity manifests itself in the uniqueness of each believer. Nobody is just like anyone else, and that is exactly by God's design. We get into trouble when we expect others to conform to our image—in dress, behavior, and viewpoints that are nonessential to the gospel. God, however, likes variety. He wants His people to nurture each other's unique contributions to the body of Christ.

And Christ's headship is what gives the body its unity. Drawing on our variety of gifts and talents, we work together to spread and grow in the Good News of Christ's kingdom. We function *inter-dependently* rather than *independently*. None of us can be or do everything. For every Moses, there was an Aaron. For every David, a Jonathan. Even Jesus chose not to operate by Himself. He called out twelve men to walk with Him in His ministry. All believers are inextricably bound to each other.

In Practice

So how does this complementary relationship between unity and diversity work itself out in the local church? It often reveals itself in the use of spiritual gifts.

> Since we have gifts that differ according to the grace given to us, each of us is to exercise them accordingly: if prophecy, according to the proportion of his faith; if service, in his serving; or he who teaches, in his teaching; or he who exhorts, in his exhortation; he who gives, with liberality; he who leads, with diligence; he who shows mercy, with cheerfulness. (vv. 6–8)

Paul mentions seven gifts here, but he seems less interested in giving us an extensive list or treatment of spiritual gifts than in urging us to exercise the ones we have.[4]

4. See Everett F. Harrison, "Romans," in *The Expositor's Bible Commentary*, gen. ed. Frank E. Gaebelein (Grand Rapids, Mich.: Zondervan Publishing House, Regency Reference Library, 1976), vol. 10, p. 130.

He begins with prophecy, which can indicate the *foretelling* of future events as well as the *forthtelling* of God's messages with deep wisdom and insight.[5] Paul probably had in mind both types of ministries in this passage. Regarding the *foretelling* ministry, Paul's words are certainly limited to the writers of the Bible, some of whom were still alive during the writing of Romans. The *forthtelling* ministry, though, still has relevance for some believers today—those gifted with an ability to communicate the truths of Scripture.

The other gifts—serving, teaching, exhorting, giving, leading, and showing mercy—represent all the other gifts, which, Paul reminds us, should be used generously, diligently, and cheerfully (v. 8).

This representative list gives a good indication of the great variety that exists in the body of Christ.[6] It also reinforces that we're not all made the same and that we shouldn't heap guilt on others for being different from what we expect. We have no idea of the heartache deep within the people around us, and we certainly shouldn't add to it with our demands. Rather, the gifts of Christ are here not only to glorify God but also for enabling Christians to help, support, and encourage one another (see also Eph. 4:12–16).

Serving others, then, is one way in which we become "horizontal Christians"—people who apply their knowledge and faith for the good of God's program here on earth. And we serve with a unified variety of spiritual gifts, graciously given to us by our Father in heaven.

Practical Applications

Let's apply these rich truths Paul has communicated in two areas: our personal life and our life within the community of the church.

Personally, we have a couple of important lessons to learn. First, *accepting ourselves precedes giving ourselves*. We have to know and accept our abilities and limitations before we can give ourselves in service to others. Self-discovery, though sometimes painful, must precede ministry in the body of Christ. And second, *giving ourselves means accepting the person we minister to*. Serving others' needs

---

5. See Barton, Veerman, and Wilson, *Romans*, p. 235.

6. For a more comprehensive study of spiritual gifts, refer to the study guide *He Gave Gifts*, coauthored by Bryce Klabunde, from the Bible-teaching ministry of Charles R. Swindoll (Anaheim, Calif.: Insight for Living, 1998).

doesn't mean that it's our job to change people. Rather, we should strive to discover their unique gifts and learn how to build them up. Ministry is not meant to tear down and discourage but to equip and encourage.

In the local church, when the collective faith and gifts are functioning properly, the church will be these things:

- *genuinely spiritual*—controlled by the Spirit so that we minister to His people;

- *spontaneous*—serving from the heart rather than from a sense of legislated duty; and

- *sacrificial*—generously sharing time, money, energy, and talent.

Are you excited about how your faith functions? Well, read on, because Paul is just getting started!

Living Insights

What would happen if one or more parts of your body stopped functioning—or, worse, began to perform functions they weren't designed to do? The results could be comical: your feet might decide to take over the job of seeing or your hands might start breathing. So much for driving a car! You'd probably draw a few smiles as you sped down the freeway with a foot out the window and your face turning blue from lack of oxygen.

The misuse of gifts in the church, however, rarely draws smiles. People get thrust into positions and ministries they're poorly suited for and end up feeling frustrated, angry, and even bitter.

What about you? Have you ever participated in a ministry that you just couldn't seem to get the hang of? What was the outcome?

_____

_____

_____

Participating in ministries for which we're not suited isn't always a bad thing. Most believers have to experiment before they find their niche; some more than others. The key to success is knowing when to move on to another ministry. As you look back on the ministries that haven't suited you, when did you know that it was time to move on? What factors led you to this conclusion?

_____

_____

_____

_____

Ideally, all of us will find a ministry that suits our unique combination of interests, gifts, and talents. Have you ministered in a way that has been effective and fulfilling? Describe those experiences, and try to identify the spiritual gifts you were exercising.

_____

_____

_____

_____

Using our gifts is one way to serve the body of Christ. When we serve, we relate to others the way God intended—in love. Throughout the rest of this study guide, we're going to discover many other ways to serve and love the body of Christ.

Chapter 2

LOVE EXPRESSED

Romans 12:9–13

Love.

Nothing else on earth can compare to it. No force or feeling. No emotion or sentiment. Nothing evokes more powerful sensations or provokes more dramatic actions than true love. It mystifies us. It hypnotizes us. It incites us to act foolishly, comically, and even heroically. It controls us, sometimes leaving us in ecstasy and sometimes crushing us in pain.

Concerning the anguish of love, Tennyson once wrote, "'Tis better to have loved and lost Than never to have loved at all."[1] Because losing a loved one can cause so much pain, many of us may try to shield ourselves from love. Like emotional hermits, we withdraw from others, building a cold, impenetrable shell around us so no one can pierce the soft vulnerabilities that lie inside. But this lonely life is more painful than the grief of losing a love.

Tennyson, unfortunately, never addressed the course of action which is even worse than never loving—the course of loving without expressing it.

How tragic is the father who loves his son dearly but cannot bring himself to tell him. How inconsolable is the daughter who loved her controlling mother, despite all the pain, but was too afraid to share the gospel with her—even when her mom lay on her deathbed. And so many more live with heartbreak or fear or loneliness. The consequences of unexpressed love are legion and devastating.

If we Christians are to reflect Christ through our love (and we are, according to John 13:35), then we need to learn how to express it. In Romans 12:9–13, the apostle Paul makes it clear that Christian love always leads to action—deliberate and purposeful expression that glorifies God and ministers to His people. This passage explains God's design—the way in which He wants believers to express their love toward one another and the world.

---

1. Alfred Lord Tennyson, as quoted in *Bartlett's Familiar Quotations*, 15th ed., rev. and enl., ed. Emily Morison Beck (Boston, Mass.: Little, Brown and Co., 1980), p. 532.

The Way of Love

What does God's way of loving look like? Commentator James Montgomery Boice points out that

> love is not some mushy emotion that embraces all, forgives all, forgets all, and requires nothing. . . . In fact, you will notice at once that in our text Paul does not even define love. He passes immediately to how love functions.[2]

And how does love function? At its heart, it is first genuine, without hypocrisy; and it is also discriminating. Let's take a deeper look at both of these characteristics.

True Love Lacks Hypocrisy

Our love must be sincere, devoid of any pretense.

> Let love be without hypocrisy. (Rom. 12:9a)

When we share Christ's love, we don't put on an act or wear a mask that hides other feelings or motives. Our love is not to be fake or selfish, but pure—we simply, genuinely, and with our whole hearts want the best for those we're loving. And that goes for fellow believers and unbelievers alike.

When we love without hypocrisy, we don't deceive others, but act and speak in truth. If we're upset with somebody, for example, we don't just smile and say, "Everything's fine!" We deal with the problem honestly and with the person gently. Paul addressed this truth in his letter to the Ephesians:

> *Speaking the truth in love*, we are to grow up in all aspects into Him who is the head, even Christ, from whom the whole body, being fitted and held together by what every joint supplies, according to the proper working of each individual part, causes the growth of the body for the building up of itself in love. (Eph. 4:15, emphasis added)

Mature, Christlike love leads us to be both honest and kind.

---

2. James Montgomery Boice, *Romans, Volume 4: The New Humanity (Romans 12–16)* (Grand Rapids, Mich.: Baker Books, 1995), p. 1591. Used by permission.

True Love Discriminates

True Christian love also leads us to discriminate between good and evil.

> Abhor what is evil; cling to what is good. (Rom. 12:9b)

Discriminate? Wouldn't that make us intolerant? Our world would have us believe so. We are constantly told that every ideology, every viewpoint, is valid and must be affirmed—no matter how outlandish, illogical, or immoral. All truth is deemed subjective, because each of us is supposed to personally determine for ourselves what is true. According to the world, there's no such thing as objective truth, no one set of standards that applies to everyone. And if we believe there is, we must be intolerant. (Interesting that those who clamor for tolerance are staunchly *intolerant* of those who don't share their views!)

God, however, opposes the world's distorted view of "tolerance." He has made it clear in His word that His standards are objective, true, absolute, and apply to everyone. There is no valid standard other than His own. And He, above all, knows the damage sin can do. It's not something to be winked at, shrugged off, or tolerated away. Evil should be hated, and good should be clung to.

Does this mean we throw stones of judgment at people we consider evil? Not at all, as Boice explains for us.

> If we love as God loves—and we must if we are Christians—then there will be things for us to hate, just as there will also be things we must love. We will hate the violence done to people by whatever name—nationalism, ethnic cleansing, racial or religious pride, war, keeping the peace, even "necessity." But we will love the humble and those who work for peace, yes, and even those who are guilty of the violence, because we will want to turn them from their ways. We will hate lying, especially by those who are in important positions—CEOs and other heads of corporations, political figures, presidents, and even ministers. We will hate what their lies do to others. Yet we will love the truth and will at the same time also love those who are lying, for we will see them as people who need the Savior.
>
> That is what love does. Love *hates* evil—an

12

intentionally strong word. But love also clings to what is good. The Greek word rendered *cling* in some of its forms means to glue. So the idea is that true love will bond us to the good. We will stick to it like epoxy.[3]

Now that we've gone to the heart of the matter and learned that real love is both honest and discriminating, let's look at the various ways in which love can be expressed.

Eight Expressions of True Love

Love has many faces, many ways to express itself. In verses 10–13, Paul shows us at least eight of them.

> Be devoted to one another in brotherly love; give preference to one another in honor; not lagging behind in diligence, fervent in spirit, serving the Lord; rejoicing in hope, persevering in tribulation, devoted to prayer, contributing to the needs of the saints, practicing hospitality.

Devotion

Paul first urges us to be devoted to each other (v. 10a). The Greek verb for "be devoted," *philostorgos*, means "family affection, tenderly loving." It speaks of the loyalty and warmth God designed family members to have for one another. This kind of love leaves room for weaknesses and imperfections, leading family members to be committed to and supportive of each other.

Unselfishness

Next, Paul entreats us to be unselfish, giving "preference to one another in honor" (v. 10b).

To "honor" someone means to value and respect them. Paul wants us to give this respect, this affirmation, to others rather than seeking it for ourselves. Christian love inspires us to honor all people—Christian and non-Christian—because they are created in the image of God. We also respect and recognize other Christians because they are our fellow heirs in Christ and because God has equipped them to contribute to the church just as He has us.

3. Boice *Romans, Volume 4*, p. 1593.

Want to know a simple way of living out Paul's words? Say "thank you" to others for their service. That little acknowledgment can go a long way.

Enthusiasm

Paul urges us toward enthusiasm in the next verse.

> Not lagging behind in diligence, fervent in spirit, serving the Lord. (v. 11)

"Not lagging behind in diligence" basically means "don't be lazy."[4] We've all had times when we've just slipped into a complacent, indifferent routine in our walk with God, haven't we? Paul wants to shake us out of that and see us become "fervent." This word in Greek, *zeō*, means "to boil, be hot." Practically speaking, Paul is telling us to be passionate and bubble over with God's love. Loving others should spill over from a true delight in serving God, not be forced out of a sense of guilt or grudging obedience.

Hope

Paul also encourages us believers to let our love bloom into hope (v. 12a). Love points our gaze into the future. Because we are Christians, we hold a confident expectation of the Lord's return and the glory to follow. When we lift our eyes from the struggles of today and ponder the coming wonder, our love will be buoyed up by the joy of our beautiful hope.

Consistency

"Love also leads believers to persevere" (v. 12b). Perseverance is simply patience in hard times. Trials and persecution come to us all, but because of God's love, we can face our tormentors with endurance. No matter what happens to us, we know that God is in control and that He will work all things together for good (8:28).

Prayerfulness

Romans 12:12c tells us that believers should be "devoted to prayer." Why? Because prayer is our lifeline to God. How else can we remain connected to His love? The Greek word for "devoted" means "to attend to it constantly." Only when we are joined with

---

4. Boice, *Romans, Volume 4*, p. 1599.

God and His comfort and power can we remain patient in suffering and rejoice in our hope.

But what does prayer have to do with love? It's in prayer that we learn to love. When we pray for those who hurt us, trouble us, makes us angry, or just plain irritate us, our hearts open and our capacity to care grows. By taking everything to God, the source of love and wisdom (1 John 4:8, 16; Dan. 2:20), we let Him deepen our understanding of others and our ability to extend our hearts in love and forgiveness.

Generosity

Paul also reminds us that love is generous (Rom. 12:13a). Let's never accuse Paul of ignoring the practical! His words in Romans, "contributing to the needs of the saints," echo the words of James:

> If a [Christian] brother or sister is without clothing and in need of daily food, and one of you says to them, "Go in peace, be warmed and be filled," and yet you do not give them what is necessary for their body, what use is that? (James 2:15–16)

The answer to James' question is clear: it's of no use at all. The world's love is grasping; when we love someone the world's way, we want them for ourselves. We want their time and their affection; we want them to meet our needs. Real love, God's love, moves us to provide for the needs of others. And those needs, by the way, are not always financial. Money may not help someone who is grieving or lonely or sick. Sometimes the best gift we can give is our arm around somebody's shoulder, our company and laughter, our gentleness. Rich and poor alike need these touches of generous love.

Hospitality

Finally, Paul urges us to love others by being hospitable (Rom. 12:13b). Just as love leads us to generously meet others' needs, it also teaches us to welcome strangers. The Greek term for "hospitality," *philoxenia*, actually means "love of strangers"[5]—people who are foreign to or different from us.

The kind of love Paul describes fights against our prejudices, our

---

5. John Stott, *Romans: God's Good News for the World* (Downers Grove, Ill.: InterVarsity Press, 1994), p. 332.

contemptible desire to exclude those whose skin color, nationality, religion, gender, age, class, even fashion sensibilities and communication styles, are different from our own. The church of Jesus Christ is to be like Jesus Christ: open and loving toward *all*. It must be a place that reflects and celebrates the rich diversity of God's creation; a place where you'd find a dark-suited businessman sharing communion with a blue-haired teenager.

Forces That Block Love's Expression

What stops us from loving others? At least three forces.

First, *fear*. Reaching out and opening our hearts to others makes us vulnerable, because people could reject us—and who likes to be rejected? So instead of taking that risk, we back off in self-protection. Also, past experiences of being burned can make us fearful of loving again. If we don't care anymore, we think, we can't get hurt or used again.

Second, *passivity*. A lot of us wait to let the other person make the first move. Instead of taking the initiative in finding out what someone's needs are, we want someone to tell us what to do. This passivity, though, effectively squelches the spontaneity and sensitivity of love.

And third, *preoccupation*. It's so easy to get wrapped up in our own lives, our own pleasures and pains, isn't it? Sometimes we get so busy with soccer practices, Bible studies, choir rehearsals, doctor's appointments, and a whole host of other obligations that we don't spend time with others anymore or take time to notice their feelings. The pursuit of our own interests drains our energy and dims our care, crowding out love.

No matter how frightening or uncomfortable it may be, if we're going to love as Christ loved—which is our calling as Christians—we need to face our fears, our passivity, and our preoccupations. And we need to let Christ's Spirit transform them into security, initiative, and involvement.

Tennyson claimed that losing a love by death was better than never loving at all. C. S. Lewis concluded that never loving was a death in itself.

> To love at all is to be vulnerable. Love anything, and your heart will certainly be wrung and possibly be broken. If you want to make sure of keeping it intact, you must give your heart to no one, not even

to an animal. Wrap it carefully round with hobbies and little luxuries; avoid all entanglements; lock it up safe in the casket or coffin of your selfishness. But in that casket—safe, dark, motionless, airless— it will change. It will not be broken; it will become unbreakable, impenetrable, irredeemable. The alternative to tragedy, or at least to the risk of tragedy, is damnation. The only place outside Heaven where you can be perfectly safe from all the dangers and perturbations of love is Hell.[6]

This side of eternity, expressing God's love to others will always be a dangerous activity. The possibility of being rejected, hurt, and betrayed abound. But the consequences for refusing to express God's love, as Lewis noted, are even worse. Those who express God's love to others impart life to their own souls as well as to the souls of others.

When we love one another with a Romans 12 kind of love, we give life and we receive life. Imagine how inviting and invigorating our churches would be if we loved each other this way!

Living Insights

Take a few moments to consider the forces that keep you from expressing God's love to others. Of the three listed in the lesson (fear, passivity, and preoccupation), which one causes you the most trouble? Try to explain why.

_____

_____

_____

_____

_____

_____

6. C. S. Lewis, The Quotable Lewis, ed. Wayne Martindale and Jerry Root (Wheaton, Ill.: Tyndale House Publishers, 1989), p. 403.

Now go back to the lesson and browse over the section describing the expressions of love. Which do you more naturally gravitate toward? Why?

_____

_____

_____

_____

_____

_____

Which expression comes the least naturally to you? Is there something about that particular way of loving that makes you uncomfortable? What do you think the reason is?

_____

_____

_____

_____

_____

_____

What can you do to begin integrating these expressions of love into the way you relate with others?

_____

_____

_____

_____

_____

_____

Chapter 3

YOU AND YOUR ENEMY

Romans 12:14–21

*E*nemy is a word that makes us uncomfortable, isn't it? After all, Christians are supposed to love others, not have enemies— except the Devil, right? Paul made that clear when he wrote, "Our struggle is not against flesh and blood, but . . . against the spiritual forces of wickedness in the heavenly places" (Eph. 6:12).

Well, that's not exactly right. In that passage, Paul wasn't telling us that we wouldn't—or shouldn't—have enemies here on earth. Rather, he was trying to help us keep a proper perspective, reminding us that whatever enemies we're confronted with have spiritual forces at their root.

This seems more realistic, doesn't it? Let's face it, we all have enemies: the boss who warns us to never bring our "religion" to work, the coworkers who look for opportunities to sabotage us, and the neighbor who thinks our yard is his dog's "potty spot."

The secular world, however, is not the only minefield. Unfortunately, we encounter enemies at church, too, as Eugene Peterson notes:

> When Christian believers gather in churches, everything that can go wrong sooner or later does. . . .
> So Christian churches are not, as a rule, model communities of good behavior.[1]

Isn't that the truth! Like it or not, not all believers will act like Christ. When we realize what a blend of upbringings, expectations, limitations, and maturity levels the church is, we'll understand how easily conflicts can arise and enemies can be made.

Enemies are a fact of life. Thankfully, though, God has given us some "rules of engagement." In Romans 12:14–21, we'll learn how to live with friends and enemies alike—and honor Christ in all situations.

---

1. Eugene H. Peterson, *The Message: The New Testament in Contemporary English* (Colorado Springs, Colo.: NavPress, 1993), p. 478.

Thinking Clearly about Romans 12:14-21

Before we examine the specifics of this passage, let's first get two general facts about it straight.

Personal, Not National

Many people think the commands in these verses pertain to nations, not individuals—that Paul was describing how countries should treat enemy states. If this were true, however, the world would be ruled by godless despots.

What if we had dealt with the Nazi regime this way? By seeking to "bless those who persecute" us (Rom. 12:14) and giving food and drink to our hungry and thirsty enemies (v. 20), we would have signed the death warrant of the Jewish race and paved the way for Hitler to rule the world.

No, the commands in Romans 12:14-21 do not apply to nations. Rather, they apply to individual believers as they interact with people around them.

Attainable, Not Idealistic

Another false view of this passage is to see the commands as upholding an unattainable, ideal standard. Proponents of this school of thought argue that it's not possible for fallible humans to obey what Paul says here. In their minds, we're not capable of paying back evil with kindness (v. 17); they think it's impossible to never take revenge (v. 19). So they teach us to view the imperatives in these verses as something to aspire to but not as something to live by.

What a cop-out! In our own strength, of course we can't live up to these standards—but we have Christ's Spirit to help us! That's why Paul could issue the struggling Christian's manifesto: "I can do all things through Him [Christ] who strengthens me" (Phil. 4:13). And he fully expected all believers to diligently pursue their sanctification. His letters are filled with commands like the one in 2 Timothy: "Be diligent to present yourself approved to God" (2:15a).

We can—and should—seek to live out the exhortations in this passage. With these issues addressed, then, let's jump into the Scriptures to see exactly what it is that the Lord would have us do.

Rules of Engagement

Not every command Paul gives in these verses deals exclusively with enemies, but all of them can give us insight into our tough personal relationships.

Resist Your Natural Human Response

The first rule of engagement:

Bless those who persecute you; bless and do not curse. (Rom. 12:14)

There's nothing like a little "warm-up" command, is there? You know, something small and easy to do, just to get us off on the right foot. "Pray once in awhile" or "smile on occasion"—something on this level would have been nice. Paul, however, hits us full force with "bless those who persecute you" —a command that contradicts every one of our natural instincts.

Yet this is exactly what Paul exhorts us to do. He calls us to resist our impulse to strike back when our enemies attack. And even more, he wants us to *bless* those who hurt us. *The Life Application Bible Commentary* explains Paul's thought.

In context, to *bless* means to not *curse*. Instead of hoping for the worst to happen to our enemies, we are to willfully hope that the best will befall them. Instead of speaking words of hatred, we are to choose to speak words of truthful good towards those intending to hurt us. Finally, we are to pray for those who we feel are preying on us.[2]

"Warm-up" command? Hardly. But it is still completely within our capabilities to live out through God's help.

Put Yourself in the Other's Place

Next, Paul widens the application of Christian behavior. From telling us how to treat our persecutors, he goes on to tell us how to treat all people:

Rejoice with those who rejoice, and weep with those who weep. (v. 15)

This is empathy at its best, the ability to identify with another

---

2. Bruce B. Barton, David R. Veerman, and Neil Wilson, *Romans*, Life Application Bible Commentary Series (Wheaton, Ill.: Tyndale House Publishers, 1992), p. 241. Used by permission.

person's feelings so that you "make his case your own and allow what has happened to him to affect you also."[3] Paul here exhorts us to engage in people's lives, to connect with them, not only in happy times, but in sad ones too.

Does this apply to our enemies as well? Christ's life certainly tells us it does. When we empathize with those who lash out at us, something amazing happens—we begin to see the world through their eyes. We tune in to their way of looking at things. We begin to relate to them and understand their attitudes and actions. We may still disagree with them, but at least we understand where they're coming from.

Try to Live Harmoniously

In order to empathize with others, we need a certain mind-set, as Paul notes in the next verse:

> Be of the same mind toward one another; do not be haughty in mind, but associate with the lowly. Do not be wise in your own estimation. (v. 16)

"Be of the same mind toward one another," indicates that Paul is referring exclusively to Christians and their relationships with other believers. After all, Christians and unbelievers can't possibly be of the same mind. The NIV translation adds a helpful nuance with their rendering: "Live in harmony with one another." Commentator C. E. B. Cranfield shows how this like-mindedness can impact non-Christians too.

> That these words refer to relations between Christians is, of course, clear. But it does not follow that Paul's main concern at this point is not really the relations of Christians with those outside the Church; for Christians' relations among themselves are by no means irrelevant to their relations with non-Christians. While it is certainly possible that Paul is here thinking simply of Christians among themselves, it seems more natural . . . to suppose that, in exhorting the Roman Christians to agree among themselves, he here has in mind specially the

3. James Montgomery Boice, *Romans, Volume 4: The New Humanity (Romans 12–16)* (Grand Rapids, Mich.: Baker Books, 1995), p. 1610. Used by permission.

effect which their agreement (or disagreement) will have on those outside.[4]

How can we apply this principle to our enemies? It depends on their spiritual condition. If they are fellow believers, we need to try to become like-minded with them, to find that common ground in Christ that will allow us to work through the disagreements and hurt feelings. If, on the other hand, our enemy does not know Christ, we need to take a different course of action—to find other areas of agreement that can serve as launching points for reconciliation. Commentator James Montgomery Boice adds that

> we should not be like those Christian crusaders who are always looking for a fight or hunting down "Christ's enemies." We are to love and win people, not root them out to beat them senseless.[5]

Our ability to live agreeably with others relies heavily on our humility. As Paul noted, "Do not be haughty in mind. . . . Do not be wise in your own estimation." If we think that we can't possibly be wrong and that others who disagree with us can't possibly be right, we will never live out Paul's command. Only those with humble, vulnerable hearts will succeed.

One small phrase in this verse should not go unnoticed. Paul says to "associate with the lowly." Christians are not to be snobs. If Jesus had refused to "associate with the lowly," would any of us have been saved? The world's standards of status and prestige and class aren't God's; He offers salvation to all, and our job is to be His ambassadors (see 2 Cor. 5:20).

Also, many people use their relationships for selfish ambition. They deliberately interact only with those who can benefit them in some way. As Christians, however, we should also be deliberate in our relationships, but for a completely different purpose. Every action we take and every word we say should contribute to our goal of glorifying God and revealing His love to everyone we meet.

---

4. C. E. B. Cranfield, A Critical and Exegetical Commentary on the Epistle to the Romans, The International Critical Commentary of the Holy Scriptures of the Old and New Testaments (Edinburgh, Scotland: T and T Clark, 1979), p. 643.

5. Boice, Romans, Volume 4, p. 1610.

Never Pay Back Evil for Evil

Paul once again narrows his focus to deal exclusively with enemies:

> Never pay back evil for evil to anyone. Respect what
> is right in the sight of all men. (Rom. 12:17)

To "pay back" evil for evil makes us participants in evil—and an evil that escalates with each exchange. "Payback time" is a bankrupt form of spiritual economics that Paul would have us never pay into in the first place. When people hurt us, we should seek to stop the harm by refusing to retaliate.

Sometimes negative commands—those that tell us *not* to do something—can be made more helpful by coupling the negative with a positive alternative. And that's what Paul does with the second half of the verse: "Respect what is right in the sight of all men." The Greek meaning of two words in this verse, "respect" and "right," will help us get to the heart of what Paul is saying.

First, "respect" in Greek is *pronoeō*, and it means to "think beforehand . . . take thought for . . . have regard for."[6] Second is "right," *kalos*, which encompasses the ideas of "beautiful, good, noble, honorable."[7] By combining these meanings, Boice interprets Paul's words this way: "Christians are to lead the way in good or right. . . . We are to be known as those who always pursue the very best."[8] Eugene Peterson supplies a different nuance in his rendering: "Discover beauty in everyone."[9] Or we could say, "Always be on the lookout for what is good in all people."

All people? Yes, including our enemies. So, to sum up Paul's thoughts, (1) negatively, we don't advance evil by retaliating with it, and (2) positively, we look for our enemy's good and support it. That's our rule of engagement, and it is a sound strategy.

Because by both doing what is right and looking for our enemies' good and supporting it, we lay the foundation for living out Paul's next counsel:

6. Leon Morris, *The Epistle to the Romans* (Grand Rapids, Mich.: William B. Eerdmans Publishing Co., 1988), p. 452.

7. John A. Witmer, "Romans," in *The Bible Knowledge Commentary*, New Testament edition, ed. John F. Walvoord and Roy B. Zuck (Colorado Springs, Colo.: Chariot Victor Publishing, 1983), p. 490.

8. Boice, *Romans, Volume 4*, p. 1615.

9. Peterson, *The Message*, p. 329.

If possible, so far as it depends on you, be at peace with all men. (v. 18)

The first half of this verse shows what a realist Paul was. He knew that we can't always "make everything OK," that we can't control other people—some people simply don't care about being at peace with us. So he advises us to fulfill *our* responsibility and value peace. Because what better way is there to establish peace than by attempting to prevent enmity?

Leave All Revenge with God

No matter how hard we try, and in spite of all our efforts to be nice and supportive, some people will still attack us. When these times come and we find it hard to resist our instinct to fight back, Paul's words offer us an encouraging truth:

> Never take your own revenge, beloved, but leave room for the wrath of God, for it is written, "Vengeance is Mine, I will repay," says the Lord. (v. 19)

Several comforting thoughts leap out from this verse. First, Paul makes it clear that evil is wrong and rightly deserves punishment. Second, he states that retribution will indeed be meted out to the guilty party. So when people do us evil, we can rest assured that they not only deserve punishment but will receive the just penalty for their actions.

Justice, however, does not belong in our hands. At the end of verse 19, Paul quotes from the Law to emphasize his point: "Vengeance is Mine, I will repay" (see Deut. 32:35). Only God, who is completely righteous and omnipotent, has the right and power to judge people. When we take retribution into our own hands, we play God.

Be Sensitive to Your Enemies' Needs and Meet Them

Finally, Paul draws a Christlike conclusion on how we should treat our enemies, giving us the final "rule of engagement."

> But if your enemy is hungry, feed him, and if he is thirsty, give him a drink. (Rom. 12:20a)

This also comes from the Old Testament, from Proverbs 25:21, which clearly exhorts us to show kindness to our enemies.

25

However, the second half of Romans 12:20, the continuation of the proverb, definitely sounds contradictory to our modern ears:

> For in so doing you will heap burning coals on his head. (Rom. 12:20b; see also Prov. 25:22)

What in the world does this mean? Some commentators suggest that our kindness causes our enemies' conscience to burn with guilt and shame.[10] Such interpretations, however, don't seem consistent with the loving tenor of the passage, do they? John Stott offers a more likely as well as insightful alternative.

> The coals are a symbol of penitence. Recent commentators draw attention to an ancient Egyptian ritual in which a penitent would carry burning coals on his head as evidence of the reality of his repentance. In this case the coals are "a dynamic symbol of change of mind which takes place as a result of a deed of love."[11]

If the goal of all our relationships is to reveal God and lead others to Him, then bringing our enemies to repentance through kindness would be one way to attain that goal. It's also a way to follow in God's steps, for earlier in Romans we learned that "the kindness of God leads you to repentance" (Rom. 2:4). So let's strive to be sensitive to our enemies' needs and meet them, because in doing this, we fulfill Paul's final command:

> Do not be overcome by evil, but overcome evil with good. (12:21)

God has certainly overcome our evil, our malignant sinfulness, with the good of His mercy and grace, hasn't He? And as His children, we are to be like our Father—not retaliating verbal slam for verbal slam, punch for punch, but letting grace and goodness have the last word. The world may say that living this way will

---

10. In ancient times, when a person's fire in their home went out, they would borrow a hot coal from a neighbor's fire to get theirs going again, and they would carry the coal in a pot on their head. In this verse, we're asked to *heap* burning coals on their heads, suggesting that we should go beyond offering grudging, minimal help, but offer an abundance of the life-giving help our enemies need— repay their evil with bountiful kindness. When their kindness runs out, you heap your kindness on their heads to get theirs going again!

11. John Stott, *Romans: God's Good News for the World* (Downers Grove, Ill.: InterVarsity Press, 1994), p. 336.

only make us doormats or neurotics who walk around with a load of pent-up anger. But how successful has the world been in triumphing over evil?

No, if we follow God's rules of engagement, He'll not only protect us, He'll also use us for His glory. And He'll make us victors, rather than victims, because our good and loving God will ultimately and eternally have the last word. As one writer summed up, "Love is the final end of the world's history, the Amen of the universe." [12]

Amen and Amen.

Living Insights

Responding to enemies God's way can be downright scary. After all, there's no guarantee that our kindness will change their feelings and actions toward us; they may continue to try to hurt us. During times like these, we need protection. In the following verses, you'll find God's promises of divine protection and purpose. Take some time to read through each passage, then jot down what each one means to you.

Psalm 32:6–7 _____

_____

_____

Psalm 46 _____

_____

_____

Proverbs 14:26–27 _____

_____

_____

12. Novalis, as quoted in *The Columbia Dictionary of Quotations,* licensed from Columbia University Press. Copyright © 1993, 1995 by Columbia University Press. All rights reserved. In Microsoft Bookshelf 98, © and ℗ 1987–1996 Microsoft Corporation. All rights reserved.

Romans 8:31–39 _____

_____

_____

James 1:2–4 _____

_____

_____

Living in this fallen world opens us up to injury and heartache. No matter what trials we face, however, God is always there with us. He knows our pain, and He promises to use all things for His glory—even our enemies.

Chapter 4

HOW TO BE A GODLY REBEL
Romans 13:1–7

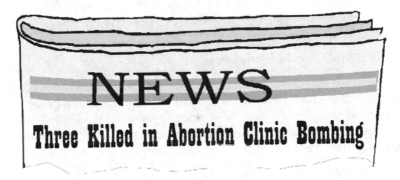

NEWS

Three Killed in Abortion Clinic Bombing

We've all seen this headline before. Sure, the details may vary—maybe the killer used a pistol instead of a bomb, or maybe he killed two or five instead of three, or perhaps it took place at a hospital instead of a small clinic. But the results are often the same: one law is broken to fight another.

Illegal actions taken in the name of "civil disobedience" perplex us because the "disobedient" faction can often persuasively justify what they've done. In the case of abortion clinic murders, the killers usually point out that they've preserved the lives of numerous innocent babies by exterminating only a few clinic workers—people whom the killers consider murderers in their own right.

We may agree that abortion is legalized murder, but can we as Christians ever condone murder in the support of life? Can we rightly advocate breaking any law if it is done with good intentions? Something inside us shudders at the thought. Yet the Bible itself condones and even promotes civil disobedience in certain cases (see Exod. 1:15–21; Josh. 2:1–7; Dan. 3; Acts 4:18–20).

What, then, are the limits of civil disobedience? When do we cross the line from civil disobedience that is God-honoring to that which is sinful? On the flip side, are we ever wrong to *not* disobey government mandates—or at least give voice to our concerns? If we condemn abortion-clinic killings but oppose abortion, for example, how can we justify paying taxes to a government that pays for abortions? Thankfully, the Bible offers us the answers.

Familiar Extremes

Before we look directly at the issue of civil disobedience, let's examine how we tend to react to our society. Let's face it, we don't live under a Christian government, and many of its actions and policies often contradict and challenge biblical values. When we find ourselves in disagreement with the government, we tend to follow two destructive extremes.

Inappropriate Independence

First, we may develop an antigovernment mentality and become militant and combative. We begin to see the government as our enemy, as the Devil's tool. We organize protests; we lead demonstrations. If we disagree with the government in any way and in any measure, we see our only option as total defiance.

Uninvolved Indifference

Or we may choose another extreme—uninvolved indifference. We remind ourselves that we're just visiting this world. We're sojourners, passers-through whose true home is heaven. This world will never get any better, we reason, until Jesus returns. So we determine to not worry at all, not vote, not pray. We conclude that we should do nothing since God will sort it out in the end.

Neither of these extremes is healthy, nor are they biblical. So how can we develop a balanced, godly perspective on how to interact with a society that clashes with God's standards?

Balanced Perspective

Before we delve into Paul's words in Romans 13:1–7, we need to remember that he was not trying to write a treatise on the biblical view of civil disobedience. Rather, he was penning a letter to a specific group of people with specific needs. He tailored his comments to fit their situation, which was quite different from Peter's and John's in the book of Acts.

Acts 4 records that Peter and John had been arrested and brought before the Jewish religious authorities for preaching the gospel. The officials commanded the two disciples not to speak or teach in the name of Jesus again (Acts 4:18). The two, however, made it clear that they could not obey the order (vv. 19–20), so they were threatened further and eventually released (v. 21). Clearly, Peter and John were godly rebels, rightly defying these

30

government-approved authorities who tried to impose a policy contradicting one of God's commands.

So the Bible *does* support disobedience in cases where human laws defy God's laws. Charles Ryrie notes:

> When civil law and God's law are in opposition, the illustrations of the Bible sanction, if not obligate, the believer to protest or disobey. But when a believer feels he should disobey his government, he must be sure it is not because the government has denied him *his* rights, but because it has denied him God's rights.[1]

We can conclude, then, that disobedience to civil authority is justified *when that authority requires us to disobey God.*

Essential Limits

The situation of Paul's readers, however, as we noted above, was the opposite of Peter's and John's. Paul was not advising believers on how to deal with *rebellious government* but with *rebellious believers,* those who refuse to submit to a civil authority operating within its God-given parameters. In essence, Paul was placing boundaries on our freedom to engage in civil disobedience.

Why We Should Obey

He begins with a strong statement:

> Every person is to be in subjection to the governing authorities. (Rom. 13:1a)

There's no wiggle room in this command, is there? Paul makes it perfectly clear *who* is supposed to do *what*—*everybody* is to *be subject* to their government.

Basically, this means that God expects all people, as a general rule, to obey the laws of their land. He wants us to obey traffic laws, refrain from trampling on the rights of others, and pay our taxes. A good Christian, then, is a good citizen.

1. Charles Caldwell Ryrie, *You Mean the Bible Teaches That* . . . (Chicago, Ill.: Moody Press, 1974), pp. 19–20.

Paul next tells us why it's so important for us to obey:

> For there is no authority except from God, and those
> which exist are established by God. (v. 1b)

We obey our government because it is supposed to serve God's purpose—to protect people from oppression and injustice and to meet the needs of the common good.

Why We Should Not Disobey

In the verses that follow, Paul uses strong terms in giving us three reasons for not resisting government. First, he tells us that *if we disobey government, we rebel against God Himself:*

> Therefore whoever resists authority has opposed the
> ordinance of God. (v. 2a)

God supports law and order, and He uses government to preserve them. Even if certain of its policies or actions violate a biblical principle, the government as a whole may still be acting according to God's design. Resisting it would then be tantamount to resisting God and His divine plan. Which brings up Paul's second point: *rebellion against God-appointed authority has its consequences.*

> And they who have opposed will receive condem-
> nation upon themselves. For rulers are not a cause
> of fear for good behavior, but for evil. Do you want
> to have no fear of authority? Do what is good and
> you will have praise from the same; for it is a minister
> of God to you for good. But if you do what is evil,
> be afraid; for it does not bear the sword for nothing;
> for it is a minister of God, an avenger who brings
> wrath on the one who practices evil. (vv. 2b–4)

A government's job entails being vigilant and aggressive in hunting down evil and bringing wrath on those who perpetrate it. Paul's use of the word *sword* invoked a vivid image for his readers. Roman officials had sabers carried in front of them as a constant reminder that they held the power of life and death (the death penalty, in those days, was usually accomplished by beheading).[2]

---

2. Craig S. Keener, *The IVP Bible Background Commentary: New Testament* (Downers Grove, Ill.: InterVarsity Press, 1993), p. 441.

Paul's words remind us that a government's ability to punish wrongdoers, even with the death penalty, is an integral part of God's plan. Believers, then, can submit to their ruling authorities with nothing to fear. Because good Christians—who obey the law and refrain from evil—have done nothing to be punished for.

Linked to good behavior is Paul's third reason:

> Therefore it is necessary to be in subjection, not only because of wrath, but also for conscience' sake. (v. 5)

Simply put, *unjustified disobedience violates our good conscience*. The best way to keep a clean conscience is to be a good citizen.

But what do we do when our government is not being good, when some of its laws cross the line from being God-honoring to God-opposing? Consider the abortion issue again, which, by the way, was also a problem in Paul's day. Roman citizens had their own ways of ridding themselves of children, as these instructions from a medical book illustrate:

> In order to dislodge the embryo, the woman should take strenuous walks and be shaken up by draft animals. She should also make violent leaps in the air and lift objects which are too heavy for her. . . . If this is ineffective, she should be placed in a mixture, which has first been boiled and purified, of linseed, fenugreek, mallow, marsh-mallow, and wormwood. She should use poultices of the same substances and be treated with infusions of old olive oil, alone or mixed with rue, honey, iris, or wormwood.[3]

These ancient techniques may seem crude, but they brought about the same brutal results. In fact, the Romans took infant killing one step further. It wasn't uncommon for an unwanted child—already born—to be left on a hillside to die of exposure.[4]

So remember, it was in this social environment, under the Roman government, that Paul wrote his command to obey civil authorities.

---

3. This was written by the Greek physician Soranus, who specialized in gynecology, obstetrics, and pediatrics in the second century A.D., in his work *Gynecology* 1.64.1–2, 1.65.1–7. As quoted by Jo-Ann Shelton, *As the Romans Did: A Source Book in Roman Social History* (New York, N.Y.: Oxford University Press, 1988), p. 27.

4. Shelton, *As the Romans Did*, p. 27.

An ungodly practice, then, even one as evil as abortion, does not give us grounds to take the law into our own hands and rebel against our government. Rather, it gives us the impetus to do everything we can to change the law—through peaceful, legal means.

Wisdom in Obedience

A government's law-enforcing authority, Paul reminds us, carries over to taxes too.

> For because of this you also pay taxes, for rulers are servants of God, devoting themselves to this very thing. Render to all what is due them: tax to whom tax is due; custom to whom custom; fear to whom fear; honor to whom honor. (vv. 6–7)

Our mandate is clear—we must pay taxes as well as all other fees, even when we disagree with the way the money will be spent. In Paul's day, taxes were used not only to build those famous Roman roads but also to build and maintain temples devoted to the worship of the Roman emperor, hardly a project Paul would have endorsed.[5] We may find some of our government's projects equally offensive, yet God requires us to support our civil authorities.

In today's complicated tax system, it's also possible for people to pay too much in taxes. Paying too much is just as wrong as paying too little. God calls us to handle our money wisely, to be good stewards of what He's given us. If we foolishly pay too much in taxes, we're taking money away from other uses God may have for it.

Personal Response

When everything is said and done, we have, basically, two commands:

- Obey God always.

- Obey government usually.

As we've noted, the only time we're justified in defying our government is when our government requires us to disobey God. By following these two rules of thumb, we'll become the kind of rebels God wants us to be: *godly* rebels.

5. Keener, *IVP Bible Background Commentary*, p. 441.

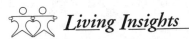 *Living Insights*

Some scriptural truths are easy to learn but difficult to embrace. Obedience to civil authorities may be one of the hardest for Christians to swallow, especially for those of us who live in democratic societies. We're given so much freedom to speak our minds, criticize our government, and lobby for our interests that sometimes the line separating appropriate civil activity and unbiblical disobedience becomes fuzzy.

Describe a situation in which you found your values clashing with an activity or policy of the government.

_____

_____

_____

_____

How does it make you feel to know that God requires you to obey an institution and pay taxes for projects that may support unbiblical practices?

_____

_____

_____

_____

What do you think is the most appropriate way to honor Christ in this situation? Why?

_____

_____

_____

_____

Paul reminds us that governments, in general, are God's appointed instruments for preserving law and order. How can this truth help you work through any conflicting feelings you may have toward government?

_____

_____

_____

_____

Take a few final moments to consider the words of Donald Barnhouse. His thoughts can help us keep a proper perspective as we live out Paul's commands:

> The believer is responsible to the Lord God Almighty, who is universally supreme. Power in every domain derives from God, but it has been distorted and debased by some of its incumbents. The Christian is to live in the midst of this world, subject primarily to God; and he is to render to the civil government what might be called a management fee, a reasonable amount for the order and protection furnished by good government.[6]

6. Donald Grey Barnhouse, God's Discipline, in Gods Covenants; God's Discipline; God's Glory (Grand Rapids, Mich.: William B. Eerdmans Publishing Co., 1964), vol. 4, p. 102.

Chapter 5

LEGAL TENDER AND LOVING CARE

Romans 13:8–10

Paul's practical instructions for Christian living display a distinct pattern. Every time he puts forward a set of applications—whether he's addressing gifts (Rom. 12), government (chap. 13), or personal convictions (chap. 14)—he always anticipates the question, *Why should we do this?* Consistently he answers, "Because that is what love does!" Paul always stays grounded in the Great Commandment spoken by Jesus:

> "'Hear, O Israel! The Lord our God is one Lord; and you shall love the Lord your God with all your heart, and with all your soul, and with all your mind, and with all your strength.' The second is this, 'You shall love your neighbor as yourself.' There is no other commandment greater than these." (Mark 12:29b–31)

In our relationships with others, nothing is more central, and nothing can accomplish more, than love. Let's join Paul in Romans 13:8–10 to learn more about love's power.

Love and Debts

As Paul segues from verse 7 into this next small section, he moves from the need to pay our public debts to taking care of our private obligations. Debts can not only sap our resources, but they can direct our energies and focus away from others as well.

Owe nothing to anyone. (Rom. 13:8a)

This statement seems straightforward enough, but unfortunately some people take it too far. They interpret this verse to mean that Christians should never borrow money—not for mortgages, not for car loans, not for anything. Jesus, however, clearly approved of loaning and borrowing, at least in certain situations (see Matt. 5:42).

So how should we interpret this verse? The answer lies in the verb *owe*. A more accurate interpretation of the Greek word might be "don't continue owing."[1] In other words, whatever debts we do owe, we should pay on time. We should be prompt in meeting our financial obligations, like mortgages, rent, loan payments, and credit cards. As commentator James Montgomery Boice sums up: "The point of Romans 13:8 is not that Christians should never borrow, but that they should never leave their debts unpaid."[2]

Obviously, paying cash outright for everything we buy is optimal. It frees our future from debts incurred today. And freedom from debt opens up opportunities to do other things with our money, such as saving for retirement or a college fund, helping the needy, and investing.

Realistically, though, with home and car and education costs what they are, few of us can do that. So, as we have need to borrow, we would be wise to avoid borrowing more money than we can afford to pay back—our monthly obligations should not surpass our ability to pay. And this can be a challenge in our day of easy credit and constant advertising to always have more and better.

James Boice addresses the problem of rampant credit abuse in our day.

> The problem for many Americans, including our government, is that debt financing has become a way of life, and those who borrow are frequently enticed, misled, or trapped into borrowing more than they are able to repay. . . .
>
> . . . Our consumer-oriented culture has deceived many people into living beyond their means on the assumption that they will have more money in the future so they can buy on credit now, enjoy their possessions, and pay later. That is a dangerous assumption, of course. We cannot count on earning more in the future than the present. But even if we could count on this, to live by debt financing is still foolish.
>
> The problem is that you not only have to repay the amount borrowed plus interest, you also have to repay interest on the interest still owed. This is known

---

1. Leon Morris, *The Epistle to the Romans* (1988; reprint, Grand Rapids, Mich.: William B. Eerdmans Publishing Co., 1992), p. 467.

2. James Montgomery Boice, *Romans, Volume 4: The New Humanity (Romans 12–16)* (Grand Rapids, Mich.: Baker Books, 1995), p. 1682. Used by permission.

as compounding. . . . If you live within your means and save, compounding works for you. A person who saves can actually become wealthy by the time of retirement, even if his or her salary is small. On the other hand, if you live beyond your means by borrowing, compounding works against you and can trap you before you are even aware of what is happening.

The biggest trap is credit cards. . . . If you have credit cards and use them only for convenience, paying the full amount due each month so that you never have to pay interest, you are in fine shape. But if you use them to borrow on time, you are headed for trouble. Unfortunately, most people use them as a revolving line of credit. . .

Consumer credit companies continue to bombard us with appeals to add just one more credit card. This is not because our credit is so good they just cannot resist wanting us as clients, but that they get 18 to 21 percent interest on whatever we fail to pay monthly, and that is much more than they can get by lending their money at today's competitive bank rates. . . .

[Ron] Blue [a Christian financial planner and author] talked to a banking friend about the way banks view people who pay credit card bills on time, thus avoiding the high interest. The banker told him that in the banking industry a person who pays his bills right away is known as a "deadbeat," because the company is unable to make much money from him. A decade or so ago a deadbeat was someone who failed to pay his bills. Now he is someone who pays his bills promptly.[3]

Using your credit cards is not wrong or bad—sometimes it is more convenient and sometimes it is the only form of payment accepted (think of hotel reservations, for example). And at one time or another most of us will be faced with emergencies, like the need for major car repairs or medical treatment, and short-term credit will be a necessity. The point is, we need to use our credit

3. Boice, *Romans, Volume 4*, pp. 1682–84.

responsibly. We are stewards of God's money, remember, and He has set us free to love and help others rather than be enslaved to our debts and the creditors who feed off them (see Prov. 22:7).

Love and Others

As we follow along with Paul in the next part of Romans 13:8, we find that the only unpayable debt that honors God is love.

Owe nothing to anyone except to love one another.

How do we "owe" love? Leon Morris clarifies Paul's thought: "'We can never say, 'I have done all the loving I need do.'"[4] Love is the Christian's way of life; we're never done loving. And our love doesn't just go out to other believers. No, Paul's command goes further than that, as commentator Robert Mounce points out:

> The obligation to love has no limit. We are to love not only those of the family of God but our "fellow-man" as well. As God's love extended to all, so must our concern reach out to believer and nonbeliever alike (cf. Matt 5:44–45).[5]

Real love extends to Christians and non-Christians, rich and poor (James 2:1–9), people of every color, nationality, age. And, we should add in these violent times, people of different sexual orientation. We don't approve of the sin, but we should still love the sinner.

Now, are we to show our love to all people in the same way? No, because different people need different expressions of love. A Christian living in sin needs "tough love," as does a strong-willed child. But try to apply that same kind of tough love to an unbeliever who lacks the power to change and you'll soon find yourself alienating people from Christ instead of attracting them to Him. As Mounce adds:

> Obviously love will take different forms depending on the recipient, but the decision to "place the welfare

4. Morris, *The Epistle to the Romans*, p. 467.

5. Robert H. Mounce, *Romans*, The New American Commentary series, (Nashville, Tenn.: Broadman and Holman Publishers, 1995), vol. 27, pp. 245–46. Used by permission.

of others over that of our own" may not be limited
to those of like faith.[6]

Love and Law

Love, as Paul shows us next, has been God's plan from the
beginning.

> For he who loves his neighbor has fulfilled the law.
> (Rom. 13:8b)

Love was the foundation upon which the Law was built.[7] God
intended for our obedience to the Law—our behavior—to be an
expression of our love for Him and others. Consider, for example,
four of the Ten Commandments that deal with person-to-person
relationships:

> For this, "You shall not commit adultery, You shall not
> murder, You shall not steal, You shall not covet." (v. 9a)

When we truly love others, we place their needs before our desires.
Because of love we will protect the sacredness of marriage and trust;
we will build up life rather than tear it apart; we will treat others
and their possessions with respect; we will hold people as more
important than things. When we show love in this way, we not
only help our "neighbor" but we honor God by fulfilling His Law.

Paul confirms the connection between love and the Law by
reminding us that all its commands can be crystallized in one
statement—or, as James 2:8 calls it, the "royal law":

> If there is any other commandment, it is summed
> up in this saying, "You shall love your neighbor as
> yourself." (Rom. 13:9b; see also Lev. 19:18, 34;
> Matt. 22:36–40)

John Stott expands on the Law-love connection.

> Law and love are often thought to be incompatible.
> And there are significant differences between them,
> law being often negative ("you shall not") and love

---

6. Mounce, *Romans*, p. 246.

7. Bruce B. Barton, David R. Veerman, and Neil Wilson, *Romans*, Life Application Bible
Commentary Series (Wheaton, Ill.: Tyndale House Publishers, 1992), p. 253. Used by permission.

positive, law relating to particular sins and love being a comprehensive principle.

. . . The truth is that love cannot manage on its own without an objective moral standard. That is why Paul wrote not that "love is the end of the law" but that "love is the fulfilment of the law." For love and law need each other. Love needs law for its direction, while law needs love for its inspiration.[8]

So, we fulfill the purpose of the Law when we obey God's commands out of love. But what does loving others "as yourself" mean? Is this a license to spend our lives focusing on ourselves first? Of course not. Now, it's true that we can't give ourselves to others very well if we don't like who we're giving. But that's not really Paul's focus here. Commentators Bruce Barton, David Veerman, and Neil Wilson help clarify his meaning.

Even if you have low self-esteem, you probably don't willingly let yourself go hungry [see Eph. 5:29]. You clothe yourself reasonably well. You make sure there's a roof over your head if you can. You try not to let yourself be cheated or injured. And you get angry if someone tries to ruin your marriage. This is the kind of love we need to have for our neighbors. Do we see that others are fed, clothed, and housed as well as they can be? Are we concerned about issues of social justice? Loving others as ourselves means actively working to see that their needs are met. People who focus on others rather than themselves rarely suffer from low self-esteem.[9]

With this kind of selfless love in mind, Paul closes with one final thought:

Love does no wrong to a neighbor; therefore love is the fulfillment of the law. (Rom. 13:10)

What a great commandment we've been given! In a world of darkness and harm, we can be agents of light and healing. Only love can accomplish this!

8. John Stott, *Romans: God's Good News for the World* (Downers Grove, Ill.: InterVarsity Press, 1994), pp. 349–50.

9. Barton, Veerman, and Wilson, *Romans*, p. 254.

Love and You

In light of the truths we've discovered in this passage, we can glean three principles to live by. *First,* only one outstanding debt honors the Lord—the debt to love others. *Second,* only one command fulfills the law—the command to love all people. And *third,* only one truth can release God's love in us—the truth that we can love others with God's help.

Jesus said, "By this all men will know that you are My disciples, if you have love for one another" (John 13:35). Let's go and show the world the marvelous love of Christ!

Living Insights

What does the balance on your love-debt look like? Have you been keeping up with your payments? Have you been making love-deposits into the emotional bank accounts of those you hold dear? Take a few moments to consider how well you're doing in this central area of the Christian life.

How have you loved your spouse lately? Have you been affectionate with and appreciative of your wife? Have you told your husband what a great guy he is? Be specific.

_____

_____

_____

_____

In what ways have you loved your children? Have you spent quality time with them? Have you been patient and understanding with them? Again, be specific.

_____

_____

_____

_____

Think of the other people in your life—parents, siblings, relatives, friends. Briefly describe how you have, or have not, shown your love to them.

_____

_____

_____

_____

_____

Did answering these questions give you a sense of accomplishment, of a "job well done"? Or do you feel a little convicted about how you've been treating your important relationships?

If you feel convicted, don't let your conviction turn into shame. Hey, none of us is perfect. Confess your complacency to God and start again right now. Ask Him to show you what you can do today or this week to express to your loved ones how much you care.

_____

_____

_____

_____

_____

Chapter 6

WAKE UP AND GET DRESSED!
Romans 13:11–14

W e are a people obsessed with time. Have you ever counted all the clocks you see in just one day? How about in just a few minutes of your day—like when you come home from work?

As you pull into the driveway of your home, you check the dashboard and see clock number one, which tells you it's 6:30 P.M. You step from the car and enter the house, but you're barely into the entryway before encountering clock number two—the grandfather clock standing by the door. In the living room you find several more: one artfully appointed clock sitting in the wall unit and another beaming from the digital readout of your VCR. When you turn on the TV, you find a fifth one next to the on-screen channel display.

In the kitchen you hit a bonanza! There's a clock on the wall and four digital readouts: on the microwave, the oven, the coffeemaker, and the answering machine.

Down the hallway you find an eleventh clock—a beautiful set of wall-mounted brass chimes that ring in symphony with the grandfather clock in the entryway. Each of the two smaller bedrooms off the hall contains a clock radio sitting on a nightstand. Your computer in the smallest bedroom also keeps you constantly aware of the time. The master bedroom has two clocks, one on each side of the bed. And don't forget the one on the bathroom sink.

As you get ready to unwind for the evening, you find one more—the one strapped to your wrist. This is number eighteen, which tells you that the time is 6:39, just nine minutes since you arrived home. You've encountered eighteen timekeepers in nine minutes, or two clocks per minute, or one every thirty seconds.

Now let's count the calendars . . .

With all our clocks and watches and calendars and daily planners (and even sun dials!), our obsession with time couldn't be more obvious. But are we measuring time correctly? Are we so focused on the hours, minutes, and seconds that we miss the epochs on God's overarching timeline?

In Romans 13:11–14, Paul urges us to open our eyes, to wake up to what time it really is. There's a new way to live in light of the dawning of the eternal day!

What Time Is It?

The Bible divides time into only two categories: "this age" and "the age to come."[1] "This age," our age, is a time of waiting for the one to come, as John Stott explains.

> The day, although it dawned at Christ's coming, has not yet experienced the fulness of sunrise at his return. . . . The apostles [knew] that the kingdom of God came with Jesus, that the decisive salvation events which established it (his death, resurrection, exaltation and gift of the Spirit) had already taken place, and that God had nothing on his calendar before the parousia [Second Coming]. It would be the next and the culminating event.[2]

Although the kingdom of God will not be fully realized until Christ's earthly reign during the millennium, it has been set in motion by His resurrection and ascension.

In light of Christ's future millennial rule, Paul sounds the alarm for us to "wake up" to God's sense of time.

Heed the Alarm

What is the first thing you do when your alarm goes off in the morning? Hit the snooze button? Paul tells us to notice instead how late it is.

> Do this, knowing the time, that it is already the hour. (v. 11a)

"Do this," he begins, but what is "this"? "This" refers to at least the preceding three verses, and at most all, of chapter 12 and the rest of chapter 13. In 13:11–14, then, Paul is establishing an end-times perspective for how Christians should live.

This perspective acknowledges that the Lord controls all events, people, and nations and that He directs history to a predetermined end. The world lives as though human history will continue forever, but we know the world is wrong. We know that we live in "the hour"—the finite period of time between Christ's ascension and

---

1. John Stott, *Romans: God's Good News for the World* (Downers Grove, Ill.: InterVarsity Press, 1994), p. 351.

2. Stott, *Romans: God's Good News for the World*, p. 352.

46

His imminent return. This unveiling of true time gave Paul a sense of urgency, a sense that all of us should have.

Our urgency, however, should not lead us into extremist ways of thinking. A doomsday mentality that sets dates for Christ's return does not stand in truth. The Bible makes it clear that no one will know the time or the hour (see Matt. 24:36).

An appropriate response is to heed Paul's exhortation to "not be conformed to this world" (Rom. 12:2). We need to remember that this world will not last forever, that one day God will judge it, end it, and replace it with a new creation (Rev. 21:1–5). Our sense of urgency springs from the realization that we only have a limited time to spread the gospel and make God known to the world.

Wake Up!

Once we know what time it is, we need to wake up and get out of bed. This is exactly what Paul commands us to do spiritually:

> It is already the hour for you to awaken from sleep.
> (Rom. 13:11b)

Paul equates sleep with spiritual lethargy, a kind of Christian couch potato syndrome. But because our time is limited, we have no time for idleness or complacency (see also James 5:8–9; 2 Pet. 3:11–14). "The hour" in which we live compels us to wake up spiritually and look expectantly for the return of Christ. Paul emphasizes this thought with his next phrase:

> Awaken from sleep; for now salvation is nearer to us than when we believed. (Rom. 13:11c)

What does Paul mean by "salvation is nearer"? Isn't our salvation secure? Do we need to live up to a behavioral standard in "the hour" in order to receive our heavenly reward? Absolutely not!

In this context, Paul used "salvation" as a comprehensive term describing our past justification, our present sanctification, and our future glorification.[3] When he says that our salvation is "nearer . . . than when we believed," he simply means that every passing moment brings us closer to the end of "the hour"—closer to our glorification. Commentator C. E. B. Cranfield explains the urgent purpose behind Paul's statement.

---

3. Stott, *Romans: God's Good News for the World*, p. 351.

The point of this sentence was to underline the urgency of the need to awake: the time of opportunity for faith and obedience was for Paul and his readers the shorter by this lapse of time.[4]

The clock, in other words, is ticking!

The Difference the Day Makes

Some of us dread the morning; we turn away from the light and burrow back under the covers. But Paul wants to pull the blankets off, get up, and get dressed in the "armor of light" (v. 12b).

The Dawning Reality

Paul reminds us of the conditions in which we live and of those to come:

The night is almost gone, and the day is near. (v. 12a)

Despite the presence of the Holy Spirit, the whole world currently lives in the night, a time in which Christ is absent and Satan is at work (2 Pet. 1:19).

But our hope is in the reality that this time of darkness "is almost gone, and the day is near." This imminent hope should embolden us to seize the moment, to help others out of the dark and into the light. People who do not have Christ, which are most people, live without hope. Everything they have to live for—pleasure and power—leaves them empty and unfulfilled.

We, on the other hand, have a glorious future to look forward to; we have our eyes on a happy ending. We also have a purpose beyond ourselves: to strive and work for the greater good of God's kingdom and glory.

We have so much to offer to a world without hope! Not only can we offer people a place in heaven—a comforting truth in itself—but we can also give them a purpose. We can give them the opportunity to contribute to God's work and to one day hear those blessed words, "Well done, good and faithful servant."

4. C. E. B. Cranfield, A Critical and Exegetical Commentary on the Epistle to the Romans (Edinburgh, Scotland: T and T Clark, 1979), vol. 2, p. 682.

Garments for a New Life

As people of the coming Day, Paul next tells us, we need to cast off the clothes of night and wear the appropriate attire for the work that lies before us.

> Therefore let us lay aside the deeds of darkness and put on the armor of light. (Rom. 13:12b)

The Christian's job—glorifying God and witnessing to the world through righteous, loving, joyful living—is best accomplished while wearing the armor of Christ. In fact, our mission is simply impossible without His protective gear.

Before we can put on our armor, however, we first need to make sure we're not wearing something else—"the deeds of darkness." Paul explains what these are in verse 13b:

- carousing

- drunkenness

- sexual promiscuity

- sensuality

- strife

- jealousy

The first four "deeds of darkness" deal with the area of morality. If we want to "wear Christ," we can't be snuggled in the velvet-lined straitjacket of sinful habits. We can't be bound by heavy drinking or pornography or materialism or any other evil vice. No, Christ's armor is a tailored fit and can only be worn by believers who have shrugged off their sinful lifestyles.

The last two deeds listed in verse 13b, strife and jealousy, seem a little out of place with the other sins, don't they? But these relational sins can be just as destructive as the others, even if that destruction is not as immediately noticeable. Unfortunately, the church tolerates these less apparent sins, as commentator Robert Mounce notes.

> Along with the more socially repugnant acts of drunkenness and debauchery we find, rather unexpectedly, quarreling and jealousy. These too are acts of darkness. Unfortunately, the church is considerably

more tolerant toward such sins. Quarreling and jealousy, while not especially polite, are more acceptable than sexual immorality. This is not to make a case for immorality but to remind ourselves that Paul placed them together as deeds of darkness.[5]

Paul intentionally coupled relational sins with more "socially repugnant" ones to make a point—to convince us that these can be just as destructive as the more "lusty" ones to our Christian mission.

So we need to take off the "deeds of darkness" and put on the armor of light in order to reveal the salvation of Christ, as Paul explains next:

> Let us behave properly as in the day. . . . Put on the Lord Jesus Christ, and make no provision for the flesh in regard to its lusts. (vv. 13a, 14)

How do we clothe ourselves with Christ? Here are four suggestions:

> *First,* we identify with Christ by being baptized (Galatians 3:27). This shows our solidarity with Christ and other Christians.
> *Second,* we exemplify the qualities Jesus showed while he was here on earth (love, humility, truth, and service). . . .
> *Third,* we train ourselves in the use of spiritual weapons: prayer, Bible study and meditation, fellowship with other believers, and other specific habits that we can learn from Jesus.
> *Fourth,* we need to train our minds not to be persuaded by our desires for gratification.[6]

Christ is with us. He is *in* us. We're not alone, and He'll never leave us. He sees what we see, hears what we hear, knows what we think. He will forgive our failings and strengthen our weaknesses. But we must be wearing His armor for Him to help us. In other words, we've got to wake up and get dressed!

---

5. Robert H. Mounce, *Romans,* The New American Commentary Series (Nashville, Tenn.: Broadman and Holman Publishers, 1995), vol. 27, p. 248. Used by permission.

6. Bruce B. Barton, David R. Veerman, and Neil Wilson, *Romans,* the Life Application Bible Commentary Series (Wheaton, Ill.: Tyndale House Publishers, 1992), p. 257. Used by permission.

☼ Living Insights

Do you remember the time when those "deeds of darkness" Paul enumerated—drinking sprees, illicit sexual behavior, bitter infighting—caused people to blush? Nowadays, rather than being embarrassed by shameful behavior, we are entertained by it on talk shows and TV programs, books and movies. Our society is not much different from Jeremiah's:

> "Were they ashamed because of the abomination
>   they have done?
> They were not even ashamed at all;
> They did not even know how to blush." (Jer. 6:15a)

Why don't we blush anymore? Probably because we've simply been desensitized. Everywhere we look—billboards, magazines, television, movies, radio, the Internet—we receive stimulation specifically designed to engage our fleshly desires and diminish our spiritual discrimination. Every day, sitcom after sitcom, commercial after commercial work to blitzkrieg our sensitivities into oblivion. And just like the addict who needs more and more drugs to get the same buzz, it takes more illicit material today to make us blush than it did the day before. Over the years, we have lost the ability to blush at all.

The answer to our problem is the same as it was for the Israelites:

> Thus says the Lord,
> "Stand by the ways and see and ask for the ancient
>   paths,
> Where the good way is, and walk in it;
> And you will find rest for your souls." (Jer. 6:16a)

The "good way" for us is to distance ourselves from the deeds of darkness, to stop consuming and meditating on smut. Our "good way"—really, our best way—is to clothe ourselves with Christ. We can regain our innocence by returning to righteousness. What will you do today to begin your journey back?

Chapter 7

TABOO OR NOT TABOO?

Romans 14:1–12

Isn't it funny how religious convictions can vary so widely among Christians? Let's invite some believers of different backgrounds to a pool party, just to see what will happen.

Out on the pool deck, our party is well under way: the hot dogs are roasting on the grill, the drinks are getting iced in the coolers, and our guests are happily visiting and laughing under a warm, sunny sky.

Suddenly events take a turn for the worse: three couples from California decide to take a dip in the pool before lunch. They toss off their sandals and T-shirts, jump into the pool, and begin tossing a beach ball around. Bill, from Alabama, practically falls out of his chair. He doesn't believe in "mixed bathing"—males and females swimming in the same pool at the same time. He quickly excuses himself and walks into the house whispering in disbelief, "What bacchanalian ritual have I stumbled onto here?"

Passing Bill in the doorway is Amber, the teenage granddaughter of Ethel, our senior party guest. Amber, in a cool tank top and shorts, is just showing up for the party, but she barely gets both feet on the deck before Ethel meets her with a bright pink, oversize beach towel in hand. "Amber dear," Ethel says, "For goodness' sake, cover yourself before you cause some poor boy to stumble!" Amber—now a pink terry cloth mummy—trudges to the first chair she can find, plops herself down, and commences to sulk.

Andy, our Lutheran guest, tries to lighten things up. He turns to Mike, a Southern Baptist, and asks, "Want a drink from my cooler?" Mike heartily accepts, and Andy raises the lid, revealing several of his favorite brands of beer. "Which one would you like?"

Mike doesn't answer, but quietly joins Bill inside the house. "What's with him?" Andy asks. "There's nothing wrong with having one dang beer!"

"Andy!" his wife exclaims, "Watch your mouth! That graphic language really bothers me."

Sound familiar? Conflicts are practically impossible to avoid when so many different convictions exist in the body of Christ. Unfortunately, we often respond to those differences the way our party guests did—with offense and alienation instead of grace and understanding. At our worst, we allow these conflicts to escalate into disputes or even church splits. The Christians in Rome were no different. In Romans 14:1–12, Paul addresses two issues that were beginning to cause division among the church members of that city. Let's listen to his counsel and learn to bridge our differences rather than widen them into uncrossable chasms.

The Background

Next to the issue of circumcision, diet and sacred days caused the most divisiveness among believers in Paul's day.[1] Despite the strong emotions these issues caused, Paul clearly considered them nonessential to the Christian faith. To describe them, he used the term *dialogismoi*, translated in Romans 14:1 as "opinions" (NASB), "doubtful points" (NEB), or "disputable matters" (NIV).[2]

Actions

Paul first addresses the issue of dietary restrictions.

> One person has faith that he may eat all things, but
> he who is weak eats vegetables only. (v. 2)

Among those with a restricted diet were Jews who struggled to break from the rituals of their past. Their concern over the proper preparation of food made it almost impossible for Jewish and Gentile believers to even share a meal together.[3] This no doubt stifled the spirit of fellowship in the young church. The Jews, though, weren't the only ones who had a problem with meat. The Gentile believers who had come from a past steeped in pagan sacrifice also worried about the nature of the meat on their plates.

> [They] carefully checked the source of their meat or
> gave up meat altogether to avoid a guilty conscience.
> This problem was especially acute for Christians who
> had once been idol worshipers. For them, such a

1. Bruce B. Barton, David R. Veerman, and Neil Wilson, *Romans*, Life Application Bible Commentary Series (Wheaton, Ill.: Tyndale House Publishers, 1992), p. 259. Used by permission.

2. See John Stott, *Romans: God's Good News for the World* (Downers Grove, Ill.: InterVarsity Press, 1994), p. 358.

3. See Barton, Veerman, and Wilson, *Romans*, p. 261.

strong reminder of their former paganism might weaken their newfound faith.[4]

But this wasn't the only issue plaguing the Roman church. Paul identifies the second bone of contention:

> One person regards one day above another, another regards every day alike. (v. 5a)

Like the meat problem, the issue of observing holy days likely arose from the differences between Jewish and Gentile believers. One commentary describes the most likely scenario:

> The believers had differing opinions about the sacredness of certain days. For example, if a Jew who once worshiped God on the required Jewish holy days were to become a Christian, he might well know that Christ saved him through faith, not through his keeping of the law. Still, when the feast days came, he might feel empty and unfaithful if he didn't dedicate those days to God. Other believers might not have any concern about that.[5]

Reactions

These differences in themselves were not a problem, but the Romans' reaction to them disrupted church life. Paul identifies the first reaction:

> Now accept the one who is weak in faith, but not for the purpose of passing judgment on his opinions. . . . The one who eats is not to regard with contempt the one who does not eat. (vv. 1, 3a)

The Greek term for "regard with contempt," *exoutheneo*, literally means "to regard as nothing, to despise utterly."[6] It describes an attitude of prideful superiority. The meat-eaters were looking down on the non-eaters and were acting like the non-eaters' views

---

4. See Barton, Veerman, and Wilson, *Romans*, p. 261.

5. See Barton, Veerman, and Wilson, *Romans*, p. 263.

6. W. E. Vine, *Vine's Expository Dictionary of Old and New Testament Words* (London, England: Oliphants, 1981), cited by *Logos Library System 2.0* under article titled "Despise, Despiser," Part A. Verbs, 1. *Exoutheneo*.

didn't matter at all. But the vegetarians were reacting in their own sinful way, as Paul goes on to show:

And the one who does not eat is not to judge the one who eats. (v. 3b)

Obviously, the abstainers had concluded that what was wrong for them was wrong for everyone.

The Groups

In light of the actions and reactions that were taking place, Paul classified the Roman believers into two groups—the *weak*, who, because of their backgrounds, had reservations about the issues of diet and holy days, and the *strong*, who had no qualms about these things (see v. 2).

The Issues

So how should Christians act when they clash over a *dialogismoi*, a "disputable matter"?

Regarding Diet

Let's first examine Paul's answer to the meat problem. Remember what he wrote in verse 3?

The one who eats is not to regard with contempt the one who does not eat, and the one who does not eat is not to judge the one who eats.

Contempt and judgment of a fellow believer who sees things differently is wrong—but why? Because "God has accepted him" (v. 3c). As Paul points out:

Who are you to judge the servant of another? To his own master he stands or falls; and he will stand, for the Lord is able to make him stand. (v. 4)

Regarding Days

Now look at Paul's words concerning the observance of holy days:

One person regards one day above another, an-other regards every day alike. *Each person must be fully convinced in his own mind.* (v. 5, emphasis added)

Paul's instructions to the Romans is just as applicable to us when we find ourselves clashing over disputable matters. First, we should become convinced in our own minds what is right for us personally. Second, we should remember that those who disagree with us are still accepted by God. Finally, we should focus more on pleasing the Lord than on pleasing other people. Paul emphasizes this point in the next verse:

> He who observes the day, observes it for the Lord, and he who eats, does so for the Lord, for he gives thanks to God; and he who eats not, for the Lord he does not eat, and gives thanks to God. (v. 6)

Whether we choose to enjoy or abstain, one principle of freedom should always guide us: we are to consecrate our actions, attitudes, and habits *to the Lord*.

Three Principles

The remainder of our passage, verses 7–12, contains three principles that can help us remove contempt and judgmentalism from our relationships with each other.

First, remember that *all members of the body of Christ are interrelated*.

> For not one of us lives for himself, and not one dies for himself. (v. 7)

It's so much easier to get along, to allow room for each others' differences, when we remember that we're on the same team, that we have the same purpose and goal—even if we pursue it a little differently.

Next, keep in mind that *all members are under one Head*.

> For if we live, we live for the Lord, or if we die, we die for the Lord; therefore whether we live or die, we are the Lord's. For to this end Christ died and lived again, that He might be Lord both of the dead and of the living. (vv. 8–9)

Championship teams have players who respect each other's roles and trust each other to obey the coach's instructions. As members of God's "team," we all submit and answer to only one person— our "head coach," Jesus Christ.

Finally, know that *all members will face judgment.*

> But you, why do you judge your brother? Or you
> again, why do you regard your brother with con-
> tempt? For we will all stand before the judgment
> seat of God. For it is written,
>> "As I live, says the Lord, every knee shall bow
>>   to Me.
>> And every tongue shall give praise to God."
> So then each one of us will give an account of
> himself to God. (vv. 10–12)

In the end, we won't be rewarded for taking the "right" sides on disputable issues, for Paul has made it clear that there is no right or wrong side. Instead, we'll be praised—or not praised—for the attitudes we've displayed and how we've treated those who disagree with us.

Do we have room in the body of Christ for those who are comfortable with their freedom, exercising it with discretion and good judgment? Do we make a place for those whose standards are stricter, being careful not to offend them or cause them to stumble? Is there room in our fellowship for those, like Andy, who drink in moderation and those, like Mike, who prefer not to drink at all? For those, like Amber, who enjoy wearing shorts and those, like Ethel, who'd rather cover themselves up? For those, like the California couples, who are comfortable with men and women swimming together and those, like Southern gentleman Bill, who are not?

According to Paul, with a godly attitude, we can find room for them all.

Living Insights

Another great passage to consider concerning gray areas is 1 Corinthians 8:1–13. Take time to read through it and to review our lesson. Then answer the following questions.

In which gray areas do you typically participate (dancing, "mixed bathing," drinking alcohol, smoking)? Do you feel you handle these freedoms appropriately?

_____

_____

_____

_____

In which gray areas has the Lord led you to abstain? Why?

_____

_____

_____

_____

Based on Paul's admonishments, when are you free to enjoy your liberty and when should you limit it for the sake of others?

_____

_____

_____

_____

How should you respond to those who enjoy more liberties than you do if they're participating in those activities with discretion?

_____

_____

_____

_____

How should you respond to them if they're flaunting their liberty or expressing it unwisely?

_____

_____

_____

_____

How should you respond to those who choose to enjoy fewer liberties than you do, especially when you are in their company?

_____

_____

_____

_____

So often, it's hard to determine which behaviors are right and which are wrong. In the end, it's a judgment call, and we're bound to make a mistake now and then. If we love one another, though, that love, which covers a multitude of sins, will also cover a multitude of mistakes (see Prov. 10:12; 1 Pet. 4:8).

Chapter 8

LIBERTY ON A TIGHTROPE
Romans 14:13–23

On a hot August morning in 1974, a little-known tightrope walker named Philippe Petit became world famous.

For forty-five minutes, he crossed and recrossed a cable stretched between the twin towers of the World Trade Center in New York City seven times. He was 1,350 feet—more than a third of a mile— above the unforgiving concrete of the street below. Making his journey even more perilous was the risk of winds funneling into the man-made canyon with little or no warning—at any minute, they could have sent him plummeting to certain death.

Afterwards, Petit tried to describe why he took such a risk:

> I feel I belong to the sky. It is the moment of purest happiness. . . . I breathe very slowly and enjoy immensely the miracle of balance. . . .
>
> I felt fear, and I fought it, and then laughed at it. I lay down on a wire with my nose almost in the clouds and listened to the noises of the everyday world fall silent until I was surrounded by complete peace. I knew the rapture of the heights.[1]

"The miracle of balance . . . the rapture of the heights"—we Christians know these too, don't we? Whether we realize it or not, we walk a spiritual tightrope every day—miraculously balancing our Christian liberty with Christlike love.

What's at stake if we take a false step at these heights? We certainly don't risk our salvation—there's a strong safety net stretched beneath us, woven with grace and forgiveness. We do, however, jeopardize the conscience of weaker believers. When we express our liberty callously, we can cause them to stumble and struggle in their faith. So how can we maintain our balance—how can we enjoy our freedom without sending others sprawling? Let's take a tightrope lesson from Paul, who, in Romans 14:13–23, shows us how to master "the miracle of balance."

---

1. Philippe Petit and John Reddy, *Two Towers, I Walk*, as quoted in Reader's Digest, April 1975, pp. 226–27.

The Correct Stance to Start With

Paul begins by describing the balanced stance that gets us off to a safe start:

Therefore let us not judge one another anymore, but rather determine this—not to put an obstacle or a stumbling block in a brother's way. (Rom. 14:13)

With all the shifting winds that whirl through this world, the last thing we tightrope walkers need is to trip each other up. Both "strong" and "weak"[2] believers can become guilty of this, as Bruce Barton, David Veerman, and Neil Wilson explain.

Both "strong" and "weak" Christians can cause their brothers and sisters to stumble. A *stumbling block or obstacle* refers to something that might cause someone to trip or fall into sin. The strong but insensitive Christian may flaunt his or her freedom, be a harmful example, and thus offend others' consciences. The scrupulous but weak Christian may try to fence others in with petty rules and regulations, thus causing dissension. Paul wants his readers to be both strong in the faith and sensitive to others' needs. Because we are all strong in certain areas and weak in others, we constantly need to monitor the effects of our behavior on others.[3]

Getting our balance means adopting an attitude of concern for others, one in which we are sensitive to their needs. *Keeping* our balance, though . . . that's another issue. Let's see what Paul has to say on that subject.

Principles to Protect Our Balance

Equipped with a balanced stance, we're now ready to take our first step onto the wire. While we're out there, we can benefit from several principles that will help us maintain our balance—pointers that will keep us from either abusing our liberty or ignoring it.

2. Let's remember that Paul, in referring to the "weak," did not mean legalists who stubbornly try to enforce their rules on everyone else. Rather, he meant people who weren't yet sure of or confident in their newfound freedom in Christ.

3. Bruce B. Barton, David R. Veerman, and Neil Wilson, *Romans*, The Life Application Bible Commentary Series (Wheaton, Ill.: Tyndale House Publishers, 1992), p. 266. Used by permission.

Nothing Is Unclean

The first principle gives us a fresh perspective on freedom.

> I know and am convinced in the Lord Jesus that
> nothing is unclean in itself. (v. 14a)

When it comes to gray areas—*dialogismoi*, "disputable matters"—
Paul makes it clear that nothing by nature is unclean (see also
Matt. 15:10–11; 1 Tim. 4:4). However, an activity may become
unclean if it is done in the wrong way or with the wrong motives,
as Paul goes on to tell us.

> But to him who thinks anything to be unclean, to
> him it is unclean. For if because of food your brother
> is hurt, you are no longer walking according to love.
> Do not destroy with your food him for whom Christ
> died. (Rom. 14:14b–15)

"You are no longer walking according to love." How
fundamental. What is a Christian without love?

Love, Paul is telling us, limits liberty. Our concern for our
weaker brothers and sisters will rein in the ways we express our
freedom. Lest we think such restrictions are too painful, Paul
reminds us that Jesus gave His life for those "weak" ones who are
"cramping our style." Who are we to destroy the work of Christ?[4]

Finally, Paul warns us that we might give freedom a bad name
if we use it in the wrong way.

> Therefore do not let what is for you a good thing
> be spoken of as evil. (v. 16)

Want to give liberty a bad rap? Simple—flaunt it. Use it
insensitively. "This liberty, however, if resented because it has been
flaunted in the face of the weak, can be regarded as an evil thing
on account of its unloving misuse."[5] What should be celebrated

---

4. The Greek word for "destroy," *apollumi*, "does not mean that we might cause our brother to
perish eternally by some sin. [Paul] means that sin is destructive and that if your actions cause the
other person to do what he or she believes to be sinful, then you are harming that person because
for him that behavior is wrong." James Montgomery Boice, *Romans, Volume 4: The New Humanity
(Romans 12–16)* (Grand Rapids, Mich.: Baker Books, 1995), p. 1769. Used by permission.

5. Everett F. Harrison, "Romans," in *The Expositor's Bible Commentary*, gen. ed. Frank E.
Gaebelein (Grand Rapids, Mich.: Zondervan Publishing House, Regency Reference Library,
1976), vol. 10, pp. 148–49.

can end up being condemned when Christians are self-righteous rather than self-sacrificing.

God, however, wants us to protect freedom's good name, to preserve its good reputation, to extol its virtues, and, most of all, to *enjoy it* by making sure that it doesn't hurt anyone else. If we practice our liberty discreetly, no one can speak of it "as evil." After all, nothing is unclean if it's handled in the proper way.

It's Not in the Externals

Next, Paul reminds us that the essence of our faith is in the condition of our hearts, not in the work of our hands.

> For the kingdom of God is not eating and drinking,
> but righteousness and peace and joy in the Holy
> Spirit. (v. 17)

God is not as concerned about our actions as He is about the motives that drive them. John A. Witmer gives us the essence of Paul's thought: "A concerned believer insists on right conduct, harmony, and joy rather than forcing his own lifestyle on others."[6]

These priorities not only please God but garner the approval of other people too:

> For he who in this way serves Christ is acceptable
> to God and approved by men. (v. 18)

In simplifying how we're to relate to others, Paul urges us to keep our eyes on this basic, godly goal:

> So then let us pursue the things which make for
> peace and the building up of one another. (v. 19)

Liberty Has Limits

Unfortunately, because our natural tendency is not to seek ways to build others up, Paul commands us:

> Do not tear down the work of God for the sake of
> food. All things indeed are clean, but they are evil
> for the man who eats and gives offense. (v. 20)

---

6. John A. Witmer, "Romans," in *The Bible Knowledge Commentary*, New Testament edition, ed. John F. Walvoord and Roy B. Zuck (Colorado Springs, Colo.: Chariot Victor Publishing, 1983), p. 494.

Our liberty regarding "disputable matters" is not nearly as important as the spiritual health of a fellow Christian. Because of this, we need to take a long, hard look at the way we enjoy our freedoms. We may still drink a glass of wine with a meal, but maybe not at the church picnic. We may choose to smoke a cigar, but not during a church softball game. Why? Because doing so could trip up believers whose convictions are different from ours.

Techniques for a Safe Crossing

How are you feeling about the tightrope? Still a little nervous? Don't worry. In addition to all the help Paul has given us already, he now provides us with two more thoughts that will help us cross that narrow line safely.

Be Considerate

Paul first reminds us of something we've been taught all our lives: thoughtfulness.

It is good not to eat meat or to drink wine, or to do anything by which your brother stumbles. (v. 21)

Being considerate is more than just using nice manners. It's learning the sensitivities of the believers around us, observing the things that make them uncomfortable, and avoiding those things in their presence.

Be Confident and Confidential

Next, Paul tells us to keep our convictions between ourselves and God.

The faith which you have, have as your own conviction before God. Happy is he who does not condemn himself in what he approves. (v. 22)

What a helpful reminder! Our convictions need to be our own—those agreed on between us and God. No one else can tell us what they ought to be; not our pastor, our spouse, or even our parents can tell us what to believe concerning disputable matters.

And sometimes our convictions are best acted on privately, as Everett F. Harrison explains.

The strong person . . . is warned to act on his confidence privately, where God is his witness. The natural explanation is that the exercise of his freedom in public would grieve the weak brother and raise a barrier between them, and this is the very thing to be avoided if at all possible. The strong is "blessed" (*makarios*, which can mean "fortunate" or "happy") in this private enjoyment of his freedom, because he is free from doubt and because no one who might be scandalized is looking on.[7]

The key to Paul's promised happiness is to be convinced of our convictions. If we waver in confusion, Paul notes, we risk more than a tainted conscience.

> But he who doubts is condemned if he eats, because his eating is not from faith; and whatever is not from faith is sin. (v. 23)

In other words, "If a Christian . . . does anything when he has doubts in his own mind as to whether it is right or wrong before God . . . his action does not spring from . . . his faith or trust in God and is therefore wrong. . . . The principle is, 'When in doubt, don't.'"[8]

The tightrope is stretched before us. Are you ready to step onto it? Before you do, stretch your hands out to either side—and keep them balanced between the poles of liberty and love.

Living Insights

When we think of disputes that arise from differences in convictions, we usually envision a crusty old legalist trying to shackle others with his ironclad rules. Perhaps the most well-known dispute, however, involved the opposite scenario. It was a situation in which a man was almost pressured into violating his own convictions for nothing more than the mere pleasure of others.

In his earlier years Eric demonstrated an unusual ability to run. He was a world-class sprinter in the longer distances. He postponed his intended departure

---

7. Harrison, "Romans," p. 150.
8. Witmer, "Romans," p. 494.

for China [as a missionary] for what he saw as an immediate opportunity to serve God in some way by representing the British empire in the 1924 Olympics. When Eric discovered that the qualifying heat for the 100 meters (his speciality) was scheduled for Sunday, he withdrew because of his personal convictions. He was forced to weigh the effect that ignoring his convictions could have on many believers who were watching him against the effect of disappointing multitudes of his countrymen whose hopes for victory were riding on him.[9]

Imagine the pressure Eric Liddell suffered! Those of us who have seen the movie *Chariots of Fire* know how the story turned out:

He held to his convictions, was replaced by another runner, and eventually ran in a longer race that did not involve the same complication. Eric won that race, much to the delight of everyone.[10]

What would you have done? What will you do if you're ever faced with pressure to compromise your convictions? Consider the powerful witness Eric had for his faith:

But even that second opportunity was not as valuable as the indelible lesson he demonstrated to the world about the importance of having convictions and standing firmly by them.[11]

Sometimes living by our convictions feels less like walking on a tightrope and more like fighting in a foxhole. At times, we may need to fight off legalists who try to suppress our freedom; and at other times, we might have to defend ourselves against people who want us to compromise our values for their selfish gain. In either case, we should always remember what we're fighting for: the freedom for which Christ died and the welfare of our fellow believers.

9. Barton, Veerman, and Wilson, *Romans*, p. 269.
10. Barton, Veerman, and Wilson, *Romans*, p. 269.
11. Barton, Veerman, and Wilson, *Romans*, p. 269.

Chapter 9

WE ARE ONE... OR ARE WE?

Romans 15:1–13

What would you do if you knew you only had twenty-four hours to live?

If you're like most of us, you just scanned your mind for what matters most to you. You may have thought of doing something that you've always wanted to try, like skydiving or bungee-jumping. Most likely, however, you thought of the people you'd really like to be with.

Unfortunately (or, perhaps, fortunately), none of us knows when the big moment will come. Jesus, on the other hand, *did* know. And He chose to spend His last free hours with His loved ones, the disciples, doing what was most important—praying. Listen to some of the words from His prayer known as the High Priestly Prayer:

> "I do not ask on behalf of these alone, but for those also who believe in Me through their word; *that they may all be one;* even as You, Father, are in Me and I in You, that they also may be in Us, so that the world may believe that You sent Me." (John 17:20–21, emphasis added)

What did Jesus find so important that He spent some of His last precious minutes praying for? *Unity.* And not just for His disciples, but also for those who would believe in Him "through their word." In other words, Jesus prayed this for *all* believers—even us today.

Are we making His prayer come true? Sadly, no. We often spend more time squabbling about our differences than we do gathered around the cross. Let's not think, though, that we're the only generation of Christians to experience this kind of splintering. Paul, in Romans 15:1–13, addressed this very issue in his day too. Let's enter his world, then, so we can learn how to transform our own.

The Unity of God's People

In the first four verses of chapter 15, Paul briefly continues his discussion of the weak and the strong as he segues into his treatment of unity.

Our Obligation

> Now we who are strong ought to bear the weaknesses of those without strength and not just please ourselves. Each of us is to please his neighbor for his good, to his edification. (Rom. 15:1–2)

Bearing the weaknesses of fellow believers is our obligation. Commentator Robert Mounce says that the term *bear* goes beyond mere tolerance or putting up with others' limitations. It requires us to care enough to personally shoulder their burdens as if they were our own. Why? Because we love them enough to want to help them toward maturity, toward their highest good.[1]

Christ's Example

Having made the guidelines clear, Paul next gives us an example to follow:

> For even Christ did not please Himself. (v. 3a)

Christ did not regard His equality with God as something to be used for His own pleasure (Phil. 2:6). He did not come as a king, regally demanding others to serve Him—which would have been His right. Instead, He emptied Himself (2:7), serving the Father's desire to save us by sacrificing Himself.

What price did Christ pay for forfeiting His own pleasures? Paul notes:

> As it is written, "The reproaches of those who reproached you fell on me." (Rom. 15:3b)

These words, quoted from Psalm 69, show that, not only did Christ give up the robes of deity and His very life—He even sacrificed His innocence in exchange for our guilt. Surely we can sacrifice a few freedoms to bring another believer to greater liberty!

Our Motivation

Christ's fulfillment of Psalm 69:9 led Paul to briefly comment about the nature and purpose of the Old Testament Scriptures.

For whatever was written in earlier times was written

---

1. Robert H. Mounce, *Romans,* The New American Commentary series (Nashville, Tenn.: Broadman and Holman Publishers, 1995), vol. 27, p. 259. Used by permission.

for our instruction, so that through perseverance and the encouragement of the Scriptures we might have hope. (Rom. 15:4)

Paul here identifies three benefits of the Old Testament. First, *it teaches us*. Just as Paul drew principles of truth from the ancient Scriptures, so we, too, can look to them for guidance.

Second, *it encourages us*. Bruce Barton, David Veerman, and Neil Wilson delineate the encouragement the Old Testament offers us.

How does the Bible encourage us? (1) God's attributes and character constantly remind us in whom our hope is based. . . . (2) The biographies of saints who overcame great obstacles give us examples of what can be done with God's help. . . . (3) The direct exhortation of Scripture calls for endurance and speaks encouragement.[2]

Closely linked to encouragement is the third benefit of the Old Testament: *hope*. God has promised a wonderful future for us, and the Old Testament—especially the Prophets—underlines, highlights, and illustrates that promise.

Paul's Application

Returning to his main point, Paul offers this prayer:

Now may the God who gives perseverance and encouragement grant you to be of the same mind with one another according to Christ Jesus. (v. 5)

Does "be of the same mind" mean Christians should never disagree? Commentator Robert Mounce offers this excellent explanation:

[Paul's] desire that [the Romans] "mind the same thing among one another" (literal translation) does not mean that they should all come to the same conclusion. That is obvious from his discussion of the weak and the strong—the conscience of each is to guide the conduct of that person. It is unity of perspective that is desired. And that perspective is that

---

2. Bruce B. Barton, David R. Veerman, and Neil Wilson, *Romans*, The Life Application Bible Commentary Series (Wheaton, Ill.: Tyndale House Publishers, 1992), p. 274. Used by permission.

of Christ Jesus, our model for Christian conduct. Think as he does. Take on his values and priorities. As each member of the church draws closer to Christ, we will at the same time draw closer to other members of the body. The experience of Christian unity produces a symphony of praise to God in which each voice blends with all others to the glory of God. It is a family affair. We, the adopted sons of God, sing praises to the Father of our Lord Jesus Christ.[3]

In God's orchestra, each believer plays a different instrument. An orchestra made up entirely of violins is no orchestra at all; there must also be flutes, French horns, kettle drums, and a host of other instruments. All these different instruments play in harmony with each other, all following the same conductor. The body of Christ is no different. Paul sums up our mission in this way:

So that with one accord you may with one voice glorify the God and Father of our Lord Jesus Christ. (v. 6)

The Example of God's Son

What are some practical aspects of unity? Paul shows us in verses 7–12.

Therefore, accept one another, just as Christ also accepted us to the glory of God. (v. 7)

Jesus accepted us for the glory of God. If that motivation was good enough for Him, it's good enough for us! How can we live this out, practically speaking? Barton, Veerman, and Wilson point out some specifics for us.

Accepting means taking people into our homes as well as into our hearts, sharing meals and activities, and avoiding racial and economic discrimination. We must go out of our way to avoid favoritism. Consciously spend time greeting those you don't normally talk to, minimize differences, and seek common ground for fellowship.[4]

3. Mounce, Romans, pp. 260–61.
4. Barton, Veerman, and Wilson, Romans, p. 276.

Paul found that Christ exemplified this unifying spirit when He brought Jews and Gentiles together in one body.

> For I say that Christ has become a servant to the circumcision [Jews] on behalf of the truth of God to confirm the promises given to the fathers, and for the Gentiles to glorify God for His mercy. (vv. 8–9a)

The inclusion of the Gentiles into God's plan of salvation would have been offensive to Jewish sensibilities, so Paul quotes from four passages in the Old Testament to prove his point:

> As it is written,
> "Therefore I will give praise to You among the
>   Gentiles,
> And I will sing to Your name."
> Again he says,
> "Rejoice, O Gentiles, with His people."
> And again,
> "Praise the Lord all you Gentiles,
> And let all the peoples praise Him."
> Again Isaiah says,
> "There shall come the root of Jesse,
> And He who arises to rule over the Gentiles,
> In Him shall the Gentiles hope." (vv. 9b–12)

Each of these passages held special significance for the Jews, as Robert Mounce explains:

> The first is found in 2 Sam 22:50 and in Ps 18:49. David vowed to praise God among the Gentiles, to sing in honor of his name. Israel was to be the instrument through whom God's redemptive work would extend to the Gentiles. The second is from Moses' great hymn celebrating God's victory over Pharaoh and his army: "Rejoice, O Gentiles, in company with his people" (Deut 32:43). The third is from Ps 117:1, where the writer called upon the Gentiles to lift their voices in praise to the Lord. Paul cited the verse in support of his position that the salvation of the Gentiles was in God's mind from the very first. It was not something he decided at a later time. Finally, Paul cited the well-known messianic

promise from Isaiah 11. The Messiah will come as a shoot springing up from the stump of David's family line. He will rule the nations, and on him the Gentiles will "rest their hopes" (TCNT). "The Gentile mission of the early church was a fulfillment of this prophecy, as is the continuing evangelization of the nations."[5]

The Provision of God's Power

Finally, Paul offers this benediction:

Now may the God of hope fill you with all joy and peace in believing, so that you will abound in hope by the power of the Holy Spirit. (Rom. 15:13)

Our Lord is the "God of hope." Isn't that great? God not only wants to give us joy and peace, but He also longs to give us abounding hope—hope that we can live as one and display to the world His unlimited love and power.

We may fear that Christianity is splintered beyond hope of repair. Humanly speaking, that's probably right. But for our God of hope, nothing is impossible (see Matt. 19:26; Luke 1:37). With the power of His Spirit, we can start building bridges of unity today. Won't you work toward making Jesus' prayer of unity come true?

Living Insights

Before an orchestra plays as one, each musician must tune his or her individual instrument. If you've ever attended a symphony and happened to arrive a few minutes early, you've heard the discordant noise of this tuning period. Without this noise, however, the music of the composition would never be as beautiful as it could be.

Many of us try to contribute to the ministry of our church with an instrument that is out of tune. We have relationships that are not at peace. We've allowed offenses to build up without resolution.

In order to tune your instrument, with whom do you need to sit down for a talk, either asking for forgiveness for a transgression you've committed or bringing to their attention a wrong done to you?

5. Mounce, *Romans*, pp. 261–62.

_____

_____

_____

Based on the fact that Jesus and Paul placed such a high premium on unity, what should be your goal in approaching this person?

_____

_____

Knowing that Jesus is our example, how will you talk to this person? What will your tone of voice be? What will you say? What will you try to achieve?

_____

_____

_____

Remember, it's not your responsibility alone to ensure the unity of the body. You can't control what other people choose to do and say; only God can change another person's heart. But by emulating Christ in both your attitudes and actions, you fulfill Paul's command to be at peace with all people as far as it depends on you (Rom. 12:18).

Chapter 10

COMPETENT CHRISTIANS
Romans 15:14–16

W hen you need help, few things matter more than competence. When your car is in the shop, for example, it helps to know that a knowledgeable and experienced mechanic is under the hood. When your loved ones are in the hospital, it's comforting to have confidence in the doctors and nurses taking care of them.

Yes, competence is important, especially when there's a lot on the line. And nowhere in life is more on the line than in our Christian faith. Back in Romans 13, Paul told us,

> It is already the hour for you to awaken from sleep; for now salvation is nearer to us than when we believed. (v. 11)

Our salvation, as those who are purchased by Christ, is nearer every day. But for those without Christ, it's not salvation that's drawing nearer. It's the abyss of eternal separation from God. In light of this, it is crucial for us to be competent Christians, able ministers of the gospel.

In Romans 15:14, Paul praises the Roman believers for three areas of excellence: goodness, knowledge, and the ability to keep each other on track. In verses 15–16, he speaks of his obedience to God's call on his life and his hopefulness of being effective in his ministry. These five characteristics will become for us the five marks of a competent Christian. Let's take a look at each of them so we can be sure that we're upholding God's standard of excellence in such a time as this.

A Brief Word about Context

Before we delve into the individual marks, let's get our bearings on where we are in Romans.

Many commentators believe that Romans 15:14 marks the beginning of the conclusion of the book. Interestingly, Paul devotes more space to his closing words in Romans than in any other of his letters.[1] Perhaps he did this because he had never visited Rome

---

1. John A. Witmer, "Romans," *The Bible Knowledge Commentary*, New Testament edition, ed. John F. Walvoord and Roy B. Zuck (Colorado Springs, Colo.: Chariot Victor Publishing, 1983), p. 496.

and wanted to establish a relationship with his readers.

In this section, the apostle makes some final observations about himself and the Romans, as well as telling of his future plans (15:14–29). He also offers a prayer, many greetings, a final warning, and a benediction (15:30–16:27). Most importantly though, as one commentary notes, "In these verses, we feel the heartbeat of Paul's missionary zeal."[2]

Five Characteristics of a Competent Christian

Let's listen to Paul's heart, then, and learn how to be competent representatives of Jesus Christ.

Full of Goodness

The first characteristic we can note is one of the fruits of the Spirit: goodness.

> And concerning you, my brethren, I myself also am convinced that you yourselves are full of goodness. (v. 14a)

The Greek term for *goodness, agathōsunē,* means more than an occasional virtuous act; it denotes goodness in plentiful supply. The term especially emphasizes moral excellence, which includes purity, kindness, uprightness, honesty, and good deeds.[3]

Do you notice what Paul is doing? He's complimenting the Romans, and he'll do it twice more before the end of verse 14. After all the negatives Paul has addressed in this letter, he didn't forget to acknowledge what his readers were doing well.

Too often we slip into a pattern of focusing on other people's shortcomings and end up ignoring their positives. We want very much for them to grow—sometimes for our own selfish reasons— and we hold out approval like a carrot on a stick. But Paul didn't withhold his approval and praise. No, he dispensed it generously— an example well worth following.

2. Bruce B. Barton, David R. Veerman, and Neil Wilson, *Romans*, Life Application Bible Commentary Series (Wheaton, Ill.: Tyndale House Publishers, 1992), p. 278. Used by permission.

3. Leon Morris, *The Epistle to the Romans* (1988; reprint, Grand Rapids, Mich.: William B. Eerdmans Publishing Co., 1992), p. 509.

Filled with All Knowledge

Not only were the Roman believers good, they were also knowledgeable.

> You yourselves are full of goodness, filled with all knowledge. (v. 14b)

Paul is using a little hyperbole here. The Romans obviously didn't know *all* things. In contrast to the term *full*, which presents the idea of being completely full, *all* indicates "the whole range of" or "every kind of" knowledge.[4] The implication is that the Romans had a firm grasp on the teachings required to skillfully fulfill their Christian duties. They didn't know everything, but they knew enough about the gospel to live it out well.

In penning these words, perhaps Paul thought of the intelligence and diligence of the Bereans.

> Now these were more noble-minded than those in Thessalonica, for they received the word with great eagerness, examining the Scriptures daily to see whether these things [Paul's teachings] were so. (Acts 17:11)

Great eagerness. Examining the Scriptures. These constitute what is necessary to become an intellectually competent Christian.

Now, our goal is not to gain information merely for information's sake. Rather, we grow in our knowledge of God's Word so that we can know Him better. And out of this deepened relationship, we will be more effective witnesses for Him.

Able to Admonish

Next, Paul tells the Roman believers that he is confident they are

> able also to admonish one another. (Rom. 15:14c)

The Greek term for admonish, *noutheteo*, means "to set right" or "to have a corrective influence on someone."[5] The Romans were apparently influencing the attitudes of their brothers and sisters through

---

4. C. E. B. Cranfield, *A Critical and Exegetical Commentary on the Epistle to the Romans* (Edinburgh, Scotland: T and T Clark, 1979), vol. 2, p. 753.

5. *Theological Dictionary of the New Testament*, ed. Gerhard Kittel (Grand Rapids, Mich.: William B. Eerdmans Publishing Co., 1967), vol. 4, p. 1019.

appropriate instruction, exhortation, warning, and correction—all with the goal of helping them amend their lives for the better.[6]

Admonishing others is sometimes necessary for their growth, but it is rarely easy or comfortable to do. Ever try to tell somebody that they're wrong or that they need to change? One poorly chosen word can be like a spark on a powder keg. In this volatile context of conflict and confrontation, we must seek to "correct the mind, to put right what is wrong, and to improve the spiritual attitude."[7] A tall order, to say the least!

How can we do it? The only way to effectively influence people toward growth and change is to engage in a loving relationship with them. Proverbs 27:6 reads,

> Faithful are the wounds of a friend,
> But deceitful are the kisses of an enemy.

Correction is so much easier to take when it comes from people who love us, people who want the best for us. And generally speaking, it's only in that context that we can effectively offer it.

Obedient to the Call

Paul now turns from his description of the Romans to comment on himself and his own ministry:

> But I have written very boldly to you on some points so as to remind you again, because of the grace that was given me from God, to be a minister of Christ Jesus to the Gentiles, ministering as a priest the gospel of God. (Rom. 15:15–16a)

Commentator Robert Mounce explains the apostle's calling:
> Paul's service as a priest of Christ Jesus was to proclaim the gospel of God. Using the language of religious ceremony, he pictured his role as that of a priest bringing an offering to God. The offering consisted of believing Gentiles.[8]

Like Paul, some of us have been called into vocational service

---

6. *Theological Dictionary of the New Testament*, p. 1022.

7. *Theological Dictionary of the New Testament*, p. 1019.

8. Robert H. Mounce, *Romans*, The New American Commentary series (Nashville, Tenn.: Broadman and Holman Publishers, 1995), vol. 27, p. 266. Used by permission.

to be missionaries, pastors, and teachers. Others He has called to be "tentmakers," to witness for Him as we make a living in non-religious professions.

No vocation is more sacred than another. A missionary is no more pleasing to God than a lawyer, a pastor no more spiritual than a plumber. What pleases God is our obedience to His call to serve in the body of Christ, whatever the role we play.

Productive in the Call

Finally, Paul adds the detail of *effectiveness for Christ*. He does all that he does

> so that [his] offering of the Gentiles may become acceptable, sanctified by the Holy Spirit. (v. 16b)

Paul's missionary work was an act of worship. He viewed the Gentile church as a consecrated, sacrificial offering that he presented to God for His acceptance and pleasure.[9]

In Paul's description of himself and the Roman believers, he has illustrated for us what competence looks like in the Christian life. Goodness, knowledge, admonishment, obedience, productiveness . . . they all add up to competent Christianity.

Whether we are old hands at the Christian faith or just tentative beginners starting out, the Holy Spirit lives in us, forming us into the picture of Christian competence that Paul and the Romans displayed. By yielding to the Spirit's power, we can become morally good. Through a study of the Scriptures, we can raise our level of knowledge. By admonishing one another, we preserve the integrity of the body of Christ. And by obeying and following our callings, we can participate in God's plan, just as Paul and the Romans did.

Living Insights

Are you fulfilling God's calling for your life? If you're like many involved Christians, you've been serving in your church for years. But are you sure it's in the way God wants you to?

If there's one area that most Christians feel in the dark about, it's God's call. Just how do you know what that is? Unlike the image

---

9. Barton, Veerman, and Wilson, *Romans*, pp. 278–79.

you might have of a bolt out of the blue or a definitive flash of insight, God usually calls us through some pretty ordinary means.

Want to put your service to a simple test? If you feel that you are having a positive influence for God in the lives of others, if your service gives you pleasure and the thought of it energizes you and awakens your passions, there's a good chance your current ministry is helping you fulfill your call. If, on the other hand, you're feeling discontented, drained, and ineffective, it might be time to consider a change. Take a moment to check the statements below that apply to you.

- ❏ I feel that I am capable of accomplishing more than I am presently achieving.

- ❏ I sense that God wants to use me in a meaningful way, but I'm not sure how.

- ❏ My frustration and confusion about not knowing just what to do makes me less confident and competent.

- ❏ I desire to be more fruitful and fulfilled, making a difference with my life.

- ❏ I feel there must be something wrong with me because I still have not been able to figure out what I should be doing.

- ❏ I wish I knew God's will for my life.

- ❏ I am often asked to do things I am not interested in doing.[10]

If you checked any of the above statements, then you should consider praying about making a change in your commitments. It's likely that your gifts and talents are being set aside or channeled in the wrong direction.

Pray for guidance and follow your heart. You'll soon find the path the Lord prepared for you to take.

10. Adapted from Bruce Bugbee, *What You Do Best in the Body of Christ* (Grand Rapids, Mich.: Zondervan Publishing House, 1995), pp. 14–15.

Chapter 11

PAUL'S MINISTRY AND PLANS

Romans 15:17–29

Paul, one of the greatest men of faith to ever live, seldom wrote much about himself in his letters. The section of Romans we're studying now, however, stands as a marked exception to that rule.

As we pick up the text in 15:17, Paul allows us a glimpse behind the curtain of his heart and mind, letting us see how he felt about his work for the Lord. He looks back on his past missionary service, putting it into perspective, and he looks forward to the possibilities that lie ahead of him.

Paul's Ministry

We all know Paul as Christianity's greatest missionary, but how did the apostle himself view his ministry? Of all believers, he certainly had the most room to brag about his achievements. Yet we also know that he was one of the most humble men to grace this earth. As we're about to see, Paul had mastered the art of balancing healthy confidence with appropriate humility.

Powerful

The Gentiles' widespread acceptance of the gospel meant a great deal to Paul. Although he refused to accept any credit for bringing them to Christ, he did express a deep sense of satisfaction.

> Therefore in Christ Jesus I have found reason for boasting in things pertaining to God. For I will not presume to speak of anything except what Christ has accomplished through me, resulting in the obedience of the Gentiles by word and deed, in the power of signs and wonders, in the power of the Spirit; so that from Jerusalem and round about as far as Illyricum I have fully preached the gospel of Christ. (Rom. 15:17–19)

The very power of God had been working through Paul, giving him a powerful ministry (as the repeated use of the word *dunamis*, "power," shows). Through Christ's enablement, Paul's ministry had spanned the breadth and width of his corner of the world. In the

80

Spirit's power, he had worked many miracles. So he did not shrink from boasting about the divinely-accomplished effectiveness of his sacred calling.

What was Paul most proud of? Not the extent of his ministry nor the signs and wonders that affirmed and spread it. No, for Paul, the most important aspect was that the Gentiles were coming to Christ and living in obedience to Him through what he said and did. His pride was not on account of what he had done but in what God had done through him.[1] As John Witmer notes,

> Anything Paul achieved that was worthy of praise had God's grace as its source, Jesus Christ as its motivation and goal, and the Holy Spirit as its energy.[2]

Pioneering

Not only was Paul's ministry powerful; it was also pioneering.

> And thus I aspired to preach the gospel, not where Christ was already named, so that I would not build on another man's foundation; but as it is written,
> "They who had no news of Him shall see,
> And they who have not heard shall understand."
> (vv. 20–21)

What a modest and succinct statement! These words, which took minutes to write and seconds to read, describe achievements that took Paul ten years of strenuous labor, including his three missionary journeys. Paul's desire to go where no one had gone before, commentator Robert Mounce explains, did not stem from

> some peculiar pride that would encourage him to go it on his own but because of his intense desire to reach the known world as quickly as possible.[3]

---

1. The relationship between Christ and His "fellow workers" is portrayed in different ways in the New Testament, and it is sometimes seen as a collaboration (1 Cor. 3:9). But Paul here shies away from describing himself as Christ's partner. Rather, he prefers to view himself as the Lord's agent or even His instrument. See John Stott, *Romans: God's Good News for the World* (Downers Grove, Ill.: InterVarsity Press, 1994), p. 380.

2. John A. Witmer, "Romans," in *The Bible Knowledge Commentary*, New Testament edition, ed. John F. Walvoord and Roy B. Zuck (Colorado Springs, Colo.: Chariot Victor Publishing, 1983), p. 497.

3. Robert H. Mounce, *Romans*, The New American Commentary series (Nashville, Tenn.: Broadman and Holman Publishers, 1995), vol. 27, pp. 267–68. Used by permission.

Paul clearly understood that his calling was unique; Christ calls different disciples to different tasks and equips them with different gifts. Therefore, we shouldn't feel guilty if we don't have the same pioneering spirit as Paul. But we can strive to be like him in embracing our spiritual passions and working toward turning our God-given dreams into reality.

To lend credibility to his pioneering work, Paul quoted Isaiah 52:15, revealing that Christ was fulfilling this prophecy through his ministry. He then went on to explain that his work, which had been very involving, had delayed his visit to the church in Rome:

> For this reason I have often been prevented from coming to you. (Rom. 15:22)

Soon, though, as he is about to explain, he will visit them on his way to the most rugged ministry field of all—Spain.

Paul's Travel Plans

As Paul told the Romans about his plans for future ministry, he specified three destinations. First, he would set sail from Corinth to Jerusalem, taking with him an offering for the church there. Second, he planned to travel from Jerusalem to Rome, even though he'd only be passing through. Finally, he'd make the trek to Spain, his ultimate destination. These plans sound like pleasant sightseeing to us, but in Paul's day, such travel was extremely risky.

> If [Paul] were to make all these journeys by ship, the first would be at least 800 miles, the second 1,500, and the third 700, making a minimum total of 3,000 miles, and many more if he were to travel some of the way by land rather than sea. When one reflects on the uncertainties and hazards of ancient travel, the almost nonchalant way in which Paul announces his intention to undertake these three voyages is quite extraordinary.[4]

Rome

Paul first mentioned his desire to eventually get to Rome.

> But now, with no further place for me in these regions,

---

4. Stott, *Romans*, p. 384.

and since I have had for many years a longing to come to you whenever I go to Spain—for I hope to see you in passing, and to be helped on my way there by you, when I have first enjoyed your company for a while. . . . I know that when I come to you, I will come in the fullness of the blessing of Christ. (vv. 23–24, 29)

Delayed for many years, Paul now seemed to believe that his visit to Rome was at hand. Why? Because his ministry "in these regions" had been completed. Does this mean that everyone had heard the gospel? No, that would have been impossible. John Stott explains why Paul felt justified in moving on.

> Paul's claim . . . to have "completed the preaching of the gospel of Christ" (REB) . . . does not of course mean that Paul had "saturated" the whole area with the gospel, as we might say today. His strategy was to evangelize the populous and influential cities, and plant churches there, and then leave to others the radiation of the gospel into the surrounding villages.[5]

Next, Paul noted that even after all the years and distractions, his desire to visit Rome had not diminished; it was a desire placed in his heart by God. But perhaps the most pressing reason for Paul's persistence was his need for "help" for his trip to Spain. Stott explains the significance of this term:

> The verb translated [help] (propempō) seems already to have become almost a technical Christian term for helping missionaries on their way. It undoubtedly meant more than good wishes and a valedictory prayer. In most cases it also involved supplying them with provisions and money, and sometimes providing them as well with an escort to accompany them at least part of the way. So the dictionary definition of propempō is to "help on one's journey with food, money, by arranging for companions, means of travel etc."[6]

5. Stott, Romans, p. 382.
6. Stott, Romans, p. 385.

But before Paul would reach Rome, he explained, he had a stop to make.

Jerusalem

The first destination on Paul's docket was Jerusalem.

> But now, I am going to Jerusalem serving the saints. For Macedonia and Achaia have been pleased to make a contribution for the poor among the saints in Jerusalem. Yes, they were pleased to do so, and they are indebted to them. For if the Gentiles have shared in their spiritual things, they are indebted to minister to them also in material things. (vv. 25–27)

The circumstances surrounding Paul's visit to Jerusalem have become a matter of wide speculation among commentators. Some believe that the Christians in that city were suffering because of famine or a lack of financial wisdom. Others contend that the term "poor" was a title used to describe the pious of Judea, most of whom lived meagerly. Still others think that Paul was acting as a "tax collector" for the mother church in Jerusalem. Through the Jewish Christians, the blessings of salvation had flowed to the Gentiles, obligating the Gentile churches to give money as "a humble, material, symbolic, demonstration of their indebtedness."[7]

Whatever the case, Paul would make the trip and offer the contributions as a demonstration of love and affection to Jerusalem from the Gentile believers, who gave with pleasure. Paul saw the trip as a responsibility to fulfill before heading out for Rome and Spain. He wanted to make sure that the gift was safely in their hands before moving on.

Spain

Ever since the writing of his second letter to the Corinthians, Paul had his eyes on Spain (see 2 Cor. 10:16). He had certainly heard a lot about that land. Even centuries before Christ, Phoenicians from Tyre and Sidon had engaged in commerce with Spain and had established colonies there. By the time of Emperor

---

7. For a further discussion of the many interpretational options of this issue, see Craig S. Keener, *The IVP Bible Background Commentary* (Downers Grove, Ill.: InterVarsity Press, 1993) pp. 445–46; James D. G. Dunn, *Romans 9–16*, Word Biblical Commentary (Dallas, Tex.: Word Books, 1988), vol. 38b, pp. 873–74; and Stott, *Romans*, pp. 385–86.

Augustus, the whole Iberian peninsula had been subjugated by the Roman army. And by Paul's time most of Spain was thoroughly Romanized, featuring even a few Jewish settlements.[8] Possibly with these settlements in mind, Paul expressed his desire to minister there:

> Therefore, when I have finished this [delivering the gift to Jerusalem], and have put my seal on this fruit of theirs, I will go on by way of you to Spain. (Rom. 15:28)

We'll probably never know if Paul made it. Some noncanonical sources (for example, 1 Clement 5:7) seem to indicate that he did, but even they cannot offer us proof. If he did make it, he must have been released from his confinement in Rome, where the book of Acts leaves him, and then resumed his missionary travels and made it to Spain before being re-arrested, incarcerated, and finally beheaded under Nero's persecution.

As Paul prepared for his travels, however, he was full of assurance, not only of making it to Spain but also of seeing the Romans and giving them a blessing in Christ.

> I know that when I come to you, I will come in the fullness of the blessing of Christ. (Rom. 15:29)

Even in something as mundane as the sharing of his travel plans, Paul's sensitivity to spiritual needs is evident. What a special minister he was!

Living Insights

In Romans 15:26–27, Paul describes how the believers in Macedonia and Achaia contributed money to the Christians in Jerusalem. We don't know how much they gave or for what reason, but we do know that they gave generously and joyfully (see also 2 Cor. 9:7).

Giving today can be difficult. It's hard to contribute generously and joyfully, because the cost of living is so high. Also, many unscrupulous charities ask for our money, and it's hard to know whom to trust. Let's face it, contributing money to the Lord often

---

8. C. E. B. Cranfield, A Critical and Exegetical Commentary on the Epistle to the Romans (Edinburgh, Scotland: T and T Clark, 1979), vol. 2, p. 769.

causes us to feel hesitant and mistrustful instead of joyful and generous! But the Bible offers us help. Jot down how the following verses reassure you as you give.

Proverbs 3:9–10 _____

_____

Malachi 3:10–12 _____

_____

Matthew 6:25–34 _____

_____

2 Corinthians 9:6–10 _____

_____

Philippians 4:19 _____

_____

Chapter 12

HOW TO MAKE PRAYER PRACTICAL

Romans 15:30–33

In light of the boldness with which Paul described his travel plans, we might think that he eagerly anticipated every aspect of his trip. But this was not the case.

Although Paul felt genuinely excited about his eventual visit to Rome (Rom. 15:23), the Jerusalem trip weighed heavily on his heart. He had many enemies in that city. The Jewish leaders despised him for leading the Jews away from the Law of Moses. They considered him a turncoat and a heretic worthy of stoning. Despite the dangers, though, Paul prepared to set out for Jerusalem. During his last visit with friends at Philip the evangelist's house (Acts 21:8), an ominous visitor arrived. Biblical biographer Charles Ball recounts the events of that night.

> Coming to the house where Paul was a guest, Agabus [a prophet] recognized the apostle; and, with a knowledge of the feeling that existed against Paul in Jerusalem, he warned him not to go. Like one of the prophets of the Old Testament, he made his warning vivid. He loosened the long, linen girdle from Paul's waist, and, stooping down, he bound his own feet and hands. While the believers gazed at him in silence, he said, "The Holy Spirit says, 'In this way the Jews of Jerusalem will bind the owner of this belt and will hand him over to the Gentiles'" (Acts 21:11).
>
> Immediately the whole group, including Timothy and Luke, beseeched him to give up his plan to go to Jerusalem. With tears in their eyes they pleaded, but their words were like waves beating upon a rock. Paul was determined. . . .
>
> So, knowing the danger ahead, Paul gathered his belongings and set his face like flint to go up to Jerusalem.[1]

1. Charles Ferguson Ball, *The Life and Times of the Apostle Paul* (Wheaton, Ill.: Tyndale House Publishers, 1996), pp. 178–79.

What a poignant scene. It's hard to imagine the determination in Paul's heart. It's hard to fathom the love he held for Jerusalem. Despite the dangers, Paul set out for the city filled with enemies.[2]

But he didn't go without help. Prior to this, Paul had finished his letter to the Romans. He had asked them to pray for him as he tried to minister in Jerusalem. At a time like this, what could be more important than prayer? From his prayer request in Romans 15:30–33, we can draw principles for how we, too, ought to pray.

Awareness of the Need

Paul first made the Roman believers aware of his needs so they could pray for him:

> Now I urge you, brethren, by our Lord Jesus Christ
> and by the love of the Spirit, to strive together with
> me in your prayers to God for me. (Rom. 15:30)

Paul was not afraid to let others know he had needs. Notice how he framed his request—he *urged* them to pray for him. *Urge*, in the Greek, is *parakaleō*, which means "to call to or for," "beseech," "summon," or "exhort." In this case, Paul is using his position as an apostle—one who speaks with almighty power in the name of God—to exhort his friends to pray.[3] His call is urgent because the gospel's spread and relations with fellow believers were at stake—this was more than a mere request.[4]

If Paul, the apostle, felt the need to boldly ask for prayer, how much more should we willingly share our needs with others? Sharing can be threatening, it's true—it can make us feel weak, insufficient, and exposed. Why? Because either our upbringing or our pride tells us that we ought to be able to handle our problems on our own. But that kind of thinking only leaves us alone and hurting, isolated from a caring community.

What we need is a quality we've seen in Paul before—humility. To reap the benefits of prayer, we have to open our hearts, admit

---

2. To find out what happened to Paul in Jerusalem, read Acts 21:17–23:35.

3. *Theological Dictionary of the New Testament,* ed. Gerhard Friedrich, trans. and ed. Geoffrey W. Bromiley (1967; reprint, Grand Rapids, Mich.: William B. Eerdmans Publishing Co., 1991), vol. 5, pp. 773, 795.

4. See James D. G. Dunn, *Romans 9–16,* Word Biblical Commentary series (Dallas, Tex.: Word Books, 1988), vol. 38b, p. 878.

our needs, and trust that others are more than willing to share our burdens in prayer.

Willingness to Get Involved

Prayer, to Paul, was not something to be entered into lightly. Notice again the last phrase of verse 30:

Strive together with me in your prayers to God for me.

The Greeks used the word *strive* to describe athletes who were pushing themselves to the limits of physical exhaustion. They also used the term for soldiers, and it is likely that this battle motif is what Paul has in mind here. The *Theological Dictionary of the New Testament* describes the unity that comes from this battle-hardened, striving kind of prayer.

In prayer . . . there is fulfilled the fellowship of conflict and destiny between man and man. In prayer one man becomes the representative of the other, so that there is here opened up the possibility of one standing in the breach for all and all for one.[5]

Paul needed more than a "quickie" prayer whenever the Roman Christians happened to think of him. He needed them to pick up a weapon and stand post, to put themselves in the spiritual line of fire, to push themselves to the limit for his sake and safety. This kind of prayer is hard work, requiring commitment and extracting a toll. To pray effectively with and for others, we need to get involved with what they're facing and pay the price for that involvement.

Preciseness of Specific Requests

Paul's prayer request also highlights one helpful rule of thumb: pray specifically.

That I may be rescued from those who are disobedient in Judea, and that my service for Jerusalem may prove acceptable to the saints; so that I may come to you in joy by the will of God and find refreshing rest in your company. (vv. 31–32)

5. *Theological Dictionary of the New Testament*, ed. Gerhard Kittel, trans. and ed. Geoffrey W. Bromiley (1964; reprint, Grand Rapids, Mich.: William B. Eerdmans Publishing Co., 1993), vol. 1, p. 139.

Paul enumerates three requests here—two apply to his trip to Jerusalem and the other to his visit to Rome. Regarding his trip to the Holy City, he has concerns about believers and unbelievers alike. In relation to the unbelievers, "those who are disobedient," Paul asks the Romans to pray that he would be rescued from them. Jews in other cities had tried to kill him before (see Acts 9:23–25, 29–30; 14:5–6, 19; 2 Cor. 11:24), so his request here is for the preservation of his life.

He also asks the Romans to pray for the believers in Jerusalem, that his "service" would be accepted by them. As we learned in the last lesson, Paul had collected money from the Gentile churches as a gift for the believers in Jerusalem. He worried that the Jerusalem believers might refuse his gift in an attempt to make a statement against Paul's gospel and his seeming disregard for Jewish law. Yet if the gift was rejected, the Gentile churches would certainly take offense, and the rift between Jewish and Gentile Christians would widen, possibly beyond repair. So Paul asks the Romans to pray that his gift would be accepted.[6]

Finally, Paul asks the Romans to pray for his trip to their city. In fact, he saw his trip to Jerusalem and his trip to Rome as inextricably linked—if he failed in the first city, he'd never make it to the second. And he knew he would need the joy and refreshment that fellowship with the Romans would bring him after his earlier journey and its possible perils.

Restfulness in God's Will

Above all, Paul trusted in God. He rested in the Lord's will, and he prayed that the Romans would do the same:

Now the God of peace be with you all. Amen. (Rom. 15:33)

Why do you suppose Paul highlights *peace* here? After all, the apostle could have chosen any number of other characteristics. He could have called God the God of power, love, omniscience, grace . . . any number of attributes would fit. So why peace?

First, Paul was probably making a final, subtle plea for peace between the Jewish and Gentile believers. The Jews had known for centuries that God loves peace. And He wants His people to pursue

---

6. See John Stott, *Romans: God's Good News for the World* (Downers Grove, Ill.: InterVarsity Press, 1994), p. 389.

it, especially with each other (see Ps. 34:14; 133). By emulating God, the Jewish believers would accept the Gentiles, and vice versa. The two would become one family. Paul communicated this idea in an eloquent way, as commentator James Dunn observes: "Paul the Jew, who is also the apostle to the Gentiles, says the Jewish benediction over his Gentile readers."[7]

Paul also used "God of peace" to remind himself and his readers to rest in God's protection and plan in light of the dangerous circumstances he would face in Jerusalem. As we've learned, the apostle's life and work were in jeopardy. Only by trusting and resting in God's protection would he be able to avoid debilitating doubts about his future.

So how were Paul's and the Romans' prayers answered? Was he rescued from the unbelievers in Jerusalem? Was his gift accepted by the Christians there? Did he ever make it to Rome?

Concerning the first request, John Stott tells us we can answer "yes" and "no"—"no" in the sense that he was indeed arrested, tried, and imprisoned. But we can also say "yes" because he was rescued from three mob attacks (Acts 21:30–32; 22:22–24; and 23:10), a flogging (22:25–29), and an attempted assassination (23:12–35).

In regard to the second request, we don't know for sure if Paul's gift was accepted. Surprisingly, Luke gives us no indication of it in his Acts narrative, although he certainly knew about it since he accompanied Paul to Jerusalem and recorded the apostle's statement to Felix regarding the nature of his visit (24:17). Chances are high, however, that his gift was accepted, because of the answer to Paul's third request.

He did indeed make it to Rome, just as Jesus had promised him (23:11). But Paul's arrival did not happen according to his plans. He arrived some three years later—as a prisoner and after an almost fatal shipwreck![8]

Can prayer be practical? You bet! The answers may not come as we expect, but as Paul's example shows, prayer is one of the most practical things we can do.

7. Dunn, *Romans 9–16*, p. 884.

8. See Stott, *Romans*, p. 390.

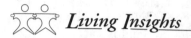 *Living Insights*

What better way to follow up a lesson on prayer than by actually praying? Before you begin, however, take a few moments to think through the issues in your life. Start by identifying the areas in which you need prayer—and remember, be specific.

In what ways do you need God's protection right now?

_____

_____

In what ways do you need God's provision?

_____

_____

In what ways do you need God's guidance?

_____

_____

How else can God help you as you try to know Him better and live for Him?

_____

_____

Now, take a moment to pray for these things. When you're finished, share them with a trusted friend or family member. As we learned from Paul's example, it's important to have others pray for us, even when our needs are small compared to Paul's. Finally, don't forget to rest in God's will. He loves you and wants the best for you. Whatever comes your way, He'll give you the strength to endure.

Chapter 13

YOU MAY KISS THE BRIDE
Romans 16:1–16

Photo albums are curious things. You either love them or hate them. There's no in-between. Why? Well, they're like pampered (and obnoxious) pets—we tend to love our own and hate everybody else's.

To us, our own photo albums are treasure troves of cherished memories permanently captured on film, allowing us to relive those special moments with the special people in our lives. What pleasure we get as we walk down the aisle again in our wedding album or tremble with fear and delight as we peer over the edge at our snapshots of the Grand Canyon!

These same albums, though, can become a source of dread and loathing to others. Who wouldn't try to slip out the backdoor when Aunt Selma comes to dinner packing slides of her vacation to Omaha? Booooooooring!

Unfortunately, many of us feel the same way about the Bible's photo albums—its lists of names—as we do about Aunt Selma's pictorial chamber of horrors! Not only can we not pronounce all those weird names, but we can't even muster up enough interest to care why they're there. When, for example, was the last time you heard a sermon on the significance of the table of nations in Genesis 10 or on the wall builders in Nehemiah 3 or even on the genealogy of Christ in Matthew 1? Most likely, it hasn't been recently.

The Bible's lists, though, actually aren't at all like Aunt Selma's snore-inducing slides. They contain rich spiritual truths— relevant truths—that we can apply to our lives. What a blessing we miss when we skip over these wonderful portions of Scripture! If we would take the time to get to know the people in these lists, we'd learn much about the kind of people God wants us to be.

Let's not miss this blessing in Romans. In 16:1–16, Paul gives us the longest list in any of his letters.[1] From his scrapbook, we'll not only get to know some inspirational people, but we'll also learn a few memorable lessons to tuck away in the photo album of our lives.

Who's Who in the Class Picture

Ever flip through one of your albums, land on your class picture, and wish to goodness that you'd written down the names of your classmates? Well, Paul remembered to do just that. In this list of fond greetings, we'll find not only names but some personal memories as well. How fitting that this letter to the Romans, after giving us so much doctrinal teaching, ends with an emphasis on people, relationships, and love.

> I commend to you our sister Phoebe, who is a servant of the church which is at Cenchrea; that you receive her in the Lord in a manner worthy of the saints, and that you help her in whatever matter she may have need of you; for she herself has also been a helper of many, and of myself as well.
> Greet Prisca and Aquila, my fellow workers in Christ Jesus, who for my life risked their own necks, to whom not only do I give thanks, but also all the churches of the Gentiles; also greet the church that is in their house. Greet Epaenetus, my beloved, who is the first convert to Christ from Asia. Greet Mary, who has worked hard for you. Greet Andronicus and Junias, my kinsmen and my fellow prisoners, who are outstanding among the apostles, who also were in Christ before me. Greet Ampliatus, my beloved in the Lord. Greet Urbanus, our fellow worker in Christ, and Stachys my beloved. Greet Apelles, the approved in Christ. Greet those who are of the household of Aristobulus. Greet Herodion, my kinsman. Greet those of the household of Narcissus, who are in the Lord. Greet Tryphaena and Tryphosa, workers in the Lord. Greet Persis the beloved, who has worked hard

1. Although some commentators have speculated that Romans 16 was not part of Paul's original letter, conservative scholars almost unanimously agree that it is an integral part of the letter. Among other things, it shows that Paul wrote this letter to real people, and he meant its truths to be applied to real lives.

in the Lord. Greet Rufus, a choice man in the Lord, also his mother and mine. Greet Asyncritus, Phlegon, Hermes, Patrobas, Hermas and the brethren with them. Greet Philologus and Julia, Nereus and his sister, and Olympas, and all the saints who are with them. Greet one another with a holy kiss. All the churches of Christ greet you. (Romans 16:1–16)

One fact jumps out upon reading this list: Although Paul had never been to Rome, he knew a lot of people there—twenty-seven mentioned by name here. How was that possible? Travel was a lot more common back then than most of us realize. Paul certainly moved around a lot, and it's likely that he came to know many people during his journeys, some of whom settled in Rome.

Without these people, Romans may never have been written. They were important to Paul. Maybe their faces came to his mind as he dictated to his scribe Tertius. And perhaps each person mentioned smiled as his or her name was read aloud during the public reading of the letter.

What can we learn from these people? They can show us that a body of believers can be diversified and unified at the same time. Let's take a moment, then, to get to know these brothers and sisters in Christ and allow them to enrich our lives as they did Paul's.

The Diversity in the Church

From Paul's list, we can see that the first-century church had a great deal of diversity. Like a garden with flowers of every color and type, the Roman church had people of different races, ranks, and genders.

Paul first mentions Phoebe (vv. 1–2), whom he commends to them, possibly because she delivered this letter to the Romans for him.[2] He calls her a *diakonos*, the term from which we get our word *deacon*. Some translators believe that Phoebe was a deaconess in the church at Cenchrea, while others contend that *diakonos* was not used as a distinct title until much later.[3] Whatever her role, we know that Phoebe was a

2. John A. Witmer, "Romans," in *The Bible Knowledge Commentary*, New Testament edition, ed. John F. Walvoord and Roy B. Zuck (Colorado Springs, Colo.: Chariot Victor Publishing, 1983), p. 499.

3. John Stott argues for the "deaconess" view in *Romans: God's Good News for the World* (Downers Grove, Ill.: InterVarsity Press, 1994), p. 393; while Leon Morris contends that the term was not yet a title in *The Epistle to the Romans* (1988; reprint, Grand Rapids, Mich.: William B. Eerdmans Publishing Co., 1992), pp. 528–29.

faithful servant of Christ and possibly a wealthy woman, as the Greek meaning of *helper* suggests—*prostatis*, "patroness, protectress."

But she was not the only person of high social status among the early Christians. Aristobulus (v. 10) most likely was the grandson of Herod the Great and a friend of the Emperor Claudius. Narcissus (v. 11), too, was a rich and famous personality who held a great deal of influence in the emperor's palace.[4]

Among these names of Rome's elite also lie those who occupied the lowest echelon of society. Ampliatus (v. 8), Urbanus (v. 9), Hermes (v. 14), Philologus, and Julia (v. 15) "were common names for slaves."[5] Yet Paul gives them just as much honor as everyone else; they are also his fellow workers in Christ, his "beloved in the Lord" (v. 8). The naturalness of his greetings gives us reason to believe that these brothers and sisters treated each other with similar honor too, no matter what their social status.

Paul's list also reveals different ethnic backgrounds. We know already that the church in Rome featured Jewish and Gentile members. Certainly Prisca (Priscilla) and Aquila (vv. 3–5a) were believing Jews (see Acts 18:2, 26), as were Paul's "kinsmen": Andronicus, Junias, and Herodian (Rom. 16:7, 11). Apelles (v. 10), too, is a Jewish name. Among the Gentiles, most of the names come from Greek, but a few are Latin: Ampliatus and Urbanus. These early Christians constituted a church that was just as much of a melting pot as our society today.

The most interesting aspect of the church's diversity, however, shows up in the large number of women greeted by Paul. Possibly ten of the twenty-seven people mentioned are ladies. In addition to Phoebe and Prisca, he also addresses Mary (v. 6), Junias (v. 7), Tryphaena and Tryphosa (v. 12), Persis (v. 12), Rufus' mother (v. 13), Julia, and Nereus' sister (v. 15). Paul gives high praise to these women. Of four—Mary, Tryphaena, Tryphosa, and Persis—he says they were "workers" or "worked hard" in the Lord. The Greek term for "worked," *kopiaō*, means "to work till one is weary."[6] That's quite a testimony— and Paul gives credit where credit is due.

---

4. Stott, *Romans*, p. 395.

5. Stott, *Romans*, p. 395.

6. Robert H. Mounce, *Romans*, The New American Commentary series (Nashville, Tenn.: Broadman and Holman Publishers, 1995), vol. 27, p. 275. Used by permission.

One woman, Junias (v. 7), receives another compliment from Paul. He describes her and her husband, Andronicus, as "outstanding among the apostles." Obviously, Paul did not mean that they were part of the Twelve, the small group of men whom Christ personally appointed and equipped to establish the church. Rather, he uses the secondary meaning of the term that designated a larger group of people sent out as missionaries from churches.[7] Since Paul himself knew a little bit about being a missionary, his praise of them as "outstanding" seems especially impressive.

The prominent place occupied by women in Paul's list shows us that the apostle held them in high esteem. Do his comments shed any light on the controversial issue of the role of women in ministry? John Stott comments:

> As we have seen, among the women Paul greets four were hard workers in the Lord's service. Priscilla was one of Paul's "fellow-workers," Junia was a well-known missionary, and Phoebe may have been a deaconess. On the other hand, it has to be said that none of them is called a presbyter in the church, even though an argument from silence can never be decisive.[8]

Whatever limitations Paul placed on women in the ministry (1 Cor. 14:34; 1 Tim. 2:12), he, at the very least, saw them as vital members of the Lord's work who were capable of great service in His name.

Men and women. Rich and poor. Jew and Gentile. The early church was the epitome of diversity!

The Unity in the Church

Not only were they noted for their diversity, but they were a beautiful example of unity that transcended differences. They made themselves a living expression of unified diversity, which Paul eloquently describes in his letter to the Galatians:

> There is neither Jew nor Greek, there is neither slave nor free man, there is neither male nor female; for you are all one in Christ Jesus. (3:28)

7. Stott, *Romans*, p. 396.
8. Stott, *Romans*, pp. 396–97.

We can find evidence of this unity in Paul's list in Romans. Four times he describes his friends as being "in Christ" (Rom. 16:3, 7, 9, 10), and five times he says that they're "in the Lord" (vv. 8, 11, twice in 12, 13). He also calls them "beloved" (vv. 5, 8, 9, 12). In addition, he describes them as "fellow workers" (vv. 3, 9) and fellow sufferers (vv. 4, 7).

These men and women were living proof that a body of believers can be diverse and unified at the same time. Their house-gatherings did not fall along social, racial, or sexual lines. No, they accepted one another and with one voice glorified the Lord Jesus Christ (15:6–7).

The same can be true of us today:

> It is of course a fact that people like to worship with their own kith and kin, and with their own kind, as experts in church growth remind us; and it may be necessary to acquiesce in different congregations according to language, which is the most formidable barrier of all. But heterogeneity is of the essence of the church, since it is the one and only community in the world in which Christ has broken down all dividing walls. The vision we have been given of the church triumphant is of a company drawn from "every nation, tribe, people and language," who are all singing God's praises in unison. So we must declare that a homogeneous church is a defective church, which must work penitently and perseveringly towards heterogeneity.[9]

Paul's final request is that the Romans would greet each other "with a holy kiss" (16:16a). This was a common practice in the early church (see 1 Cor. 16:20; 2 Cor. 13:12; 1 Thess. 5:26; 1 Pet. 5:14). But a kiss meant something quite different in that day. To Paul and his contemporaries, a kiss was a sign of affection, honor, or respect. In fact, a formal kiss became a part of early Christian worship services, usually accompanied with communion.[10] Since Paul knew that his

9. Stott, *Romans*, pp. 397–98.

10. Donald K. McKim, "Kiss," in *The International Standard Bible Encyclopedia*, rev. ed., gen. ed. Geoffrey W. Bromiley (1986; reprint, Grand Rapids, Mich.: William B. Eerdmans Publishing Co., 1987), vol. 3, pp. 43, 44.

letter would be read aloud in the church assembly, he probably inserted the command here so that the congregants would kiss each other upon the conclusion of its reading.[11]

Unfortunately, as time went on, the practice became abused. Church father Clement of Alexandria wrote, "Love is judged not in a kiss but in good will. Some do nothing but fill the Churches with noise of kissing"![12] So kissing was regulated and eventually ceased to be part of worship.

Although we don't kiss each other today, the spiritual act of showing honor to each other should definitely continue. A handshake, for example, can show a unity that transcends our diversity. In this way, we can "kiss the Bride."

Living Insights

If Paul were sending a letter to your church, how do you think he would greet you? We've seen in Romans 16:1–15 that he didn't hold back praise from those who were worthy. But he was no flatterer either. If someone was doing wrong, he laid it on the line, pulling no punches (see 2 Tim. 4:10–15).

So, applying a Pauline kind of honesty, look for the things you do well and those areas in which you can improve. Write a few sentences on what you see.

_____

_____

_____

_____

_____

_____

_____

11. James D. G. Dunn, *Romans 9–16*, The Word Biblical Commentary series (Dallas, Tex.: Word Books, Publishers, 1988), vol. 38b, p. 899.

12. McKim, "Kiss," p. 44.

_____

_____

_____

_____

Is there anything in that description you'd like to change? Take heart; God loves and accepts you just the way you are. In fact, He couldn't love you any more than He does right now. If you want to change, then, you have everything you need to live a godly life. Just ask for God's help. He's only a prayer away.

Chapter 14

WHEN TROUBLE IS BREWING
Romans 16:17–19a

We don't hear much about false teachers today. Why? Because society tells us that there is no such thing as a "false" teacher. How can people say such a thing? It's easy; they simply twist the meaning of *tolerance*. The word used to mean that we made room for others' different views. We championed our own beliefs but did not attack those who disagreed with us.

Today, however, *tolerance* means that we must accept all views as equally valid, and thus no belief system can claim to be right. As a result, there is no good reason to champion our own beliefs and there's no such thing as a false belief or a false teacher.

Paul could not have disagreed more. In Romans 16:17–19a, he warns his readers to beware of false teachers. As we'll see, these teachers were smooth talkers with an appealing message, but they brought dissension and destruction to the body of Christ.

We, too, need to examine and heed Paul's warning. False teachers abound today—they're on television, radio, and in our bookstores. With so many teachers and preachers out there, how can we know whose teaching is true and whose is false? By following Paul's sage advice, we can identify and steer clear of the false teachers of our day.

Paul Warns of Trouble

We don't know exactly what kind of false teachers were walking around in Rome. Actually, we're not even sure that they had made it there yet.[1] We do know, however, that unbiblical teachers were constantly trying to infiltrate the early church.[2] Paul himself fought them many times, attacking their heresies vigorously in the

---

1. Everett F. Harrison, "Romans," in *The Expositor's Bible Commentary*, gen. ed. Frank E. Gaebelein (Grand Rapids, Mich.: Zondervan Publishing House, Regency Reference Library, 1976), vol. 10, p. 167.

2. Robert H. Mounce, *Romans*, The New American Commentary series (Nashville, Tenn.: Broadman and Holman Publishers, 1995), vol. 27, p. 278. Used by Permission.

churches at Corinth, Galatia, Ephesus, Philippi, Colossae, and Thessalonica. He certainly didn't want to leave Rome vulnerable either. So, although we don't know the exact nature of the false doctrines, we do know what effect they were having.

Dissensions

First, Paul cautions the Romans:

> Now I urge you, brethren, keep your eye on those who cause dissensions. (Rom. 16:17a)

The Greek term for *dissensions*, *dichostasia*, is used only one other time in the New Testament—in Galatians:

> Now the deeds of the flesh are evident, which are: immorality, impurity, sensuality, idolatry, sorcery, enmities, strife, jealousy, outbursts of anger, disputes, dissensions, factions, envying, drunkenness, carousing, and things like these. (5:19–21a)

Dissension literally means "division," "disunity," and "contention." In both Galatians and Romans it takes on the connotation of a "political revolt" or "party dissension."[3] Obviously, the false teachers were causing church members to form competing factions. These teachers were dividing the church and draining of its power and witness.

This kind of divide-and-conquer tactic is especially hated by God. In addition to the sinful cousins it's listed with above, Solomon places dissensions in a distinct family of seven:

> There are six things which the Lord hates,
> Yes, seven which are an abomination to Him:
> Haughty eyes, a lying tongue,
> And hands that shed innocent blood,
> A heart that devises wicked plans,
> Feet that run rapidly to evil,
> A false witness who utters lies,
> And one who spreads strife among brothers.
> (Prov. 6:16–19)

---

3. Gerhard Kittel, ed., *Theological Dictionary of the New Testament*, trans. and ed. Geoffrey W. Bromiley (1964; reprint, Grand Rapids, Mich.: William B. Eerdmans Publishing Co., 1993), vol. 1, p. 514.

The Bible clearly places dissensions, or "strife among brothers," at the top of its "most wanted" list. Paul certainly sees it as a high-priority threat to the faith.

Hindrances

The false teachers were also causing hindrances.

> Now I urge you, brethren, keep your eye on those who cause dissensions and hindrances contrary to the teaching which you learned, and turn away from them. (Rom. 16:17)

From this English translation, it's hard to detect the rich imagery behind the word *hindrances*. The Greek word is *skandalon*, and it "denotes the bait stick of a trap, the stick that triggers off the trapping mechanism when dislodged by a bird or beast. This obviously means trouble for the trapped, and the word is used generally for trouble."[4] The false teachers, then, were setting traps for the believers, hoping to make them stumble in their faith.

Bruce Barton, David Veerman, and Neil Wilson suggest that such teachers were most likely attacking the centrality and reality of Jesus' life, death, and resurrection. Doubt was probably cast on His full humanity and total deity. With Jesus' authority undermined, an authoritative moral standard could also be eroded. And immorality was the snare that would catch and bind gullible believers.[5]

Interestingly, the identity of Jesus Christ is one of the first things a cult leader changes.[6] Perhaps these false teachers, with their emphasis on dissension, were seeking to create their own cult by trapping some of the young and weak among the Christian flock.

Why Trouble Was Happening

Paul had confronted false teachers in city after city. He not only understood the destructive nature of their false doctrines, but he also knew their motives and methods.

4. Leon Morris, *The Epistle to the Romans* (1988; reprint, Grand Rapids, Mich.: William B. Eerdmans Publishing Co., 1992), p. 376.

5. Bruce B. Barton, David R. Veerman, and Neil Wilson, *Romans*, Life Application Bible Commentary series (Wheaton, Ill.: Tyndale House Publishers, 1992), p. 293. Used by Permission.

6. Bob Larson, *Larson's New Book of Cults* (Wheaton, Ill.: Tyndale House Publishers, 1989), pp. 21–23.

Selfish Appetites

He first describes their selfish motives:

> For such men are slaves, not of our Lord Christ but of their own appetites. (v. 18a)

Paul also refers to false teachers' "appetites" in Philippians, where he writes,

> For many walk, of whom I often told you, and now tell you even weeping, that they are enemies of the cross of Christ, whose end is destruction, whose god is their appetite, and whose glory is in their shame, who set their minds on earthly things. (3:18–19)

"Appetites" here and in Romans literally means their own "bellies." These false teachers had a voracious, animalistic need to satiate their own desires. They were motivated to teach, not by a sincere faith and love of the brethren, but by a desire to make money and to grab power and prestige for themselves.

Also, it's important to note that false teachers were much more than simpletons who unknowingly taught false doctrine. They were much more sinister than that. They deliberately set out to deceive the body of Christ (compare 1 Tim. 6:3–5), and as we're about to see, they were very good at it.

Deception

Paul notes their method:

> By their smooth and flattering speech they deceive the hearts of the unsuspecting. (Rom. 16:18b)

Paul's choice of words in this verse would have raised the eyebrows of many in his audience. The term *smooth* describes the speech of a person who "speaks well and does ill."[7] It denotes "the language of a good man hypocritically used by a bad man."[8]

"Flattering speech" would have caused no less surprise. This phrase is used fourteen times in the New Testament,[9] and every

---

7. Morris, *The Epistle to the Romans*, p. 540.

8. Morris, *The Epistle to the Romans*, p. 540.

9. Mounce, *Romans*, p. 279.

other time it means "praise" or "blessing."[10] Paul, in other words, was using a term normally reserved for good people and good things to describe false teachers.

Why did Paul do this? He wanted to convey a disturbing truth: False teachers look and sound a lot like good and reliable teachers of the gospel. It would take a discriminating mind to distinguish between the two. Unfortunately, many Christians were falling prey to them. Paul writes, "They deceive." He doesn't say that they try or hope to deceive. The false teachers were succeeding—because some Christians were "unsuspecting."

A number of believers were naïve, guileless, innocent, maybe a little shallow-minded. Their innocence, however, did not come from a reasoned understanding of good and evil but from a lack of thinking things through. As a result, they were vulnerable to the subtle schemes of deceivers.

How Trouble Can Be Overcome

False teachers can be difficult to spot—difficult . . . but not impossible. Paul spells out clearly what Christians must do to stand against them.

First, we need to *keep an eye on false teachers* (v. 17a). The Greek term for "keep your eye on," *skopeō*, is a strong word.[11] It means that we must scrutinize everyone's teaching to make sure that it measures up to Bible truth.

Second, we need to *"turn away from them"* (v. 17b). We must resolve to not associate with or encourage false teachers in any way. We've got to keep them out of our midst.

Finally, Paul tells us to *"be wise in what is good and innocent in what is evil"* (v. 19). The term for *innocent, akeraious*, means "pure" and is used to describe wine that is undiluted.[12]

These words can mean just as much to us today as they did to the Romans. In a culture that increasingly reveals the active presence of spiritual forces at war against the church (Rev. 12:17), it is critical that we live lives of uncompromising holiness. Paul never intended us to become intimate with evil in order to communicate the gospel

---

10. Morris, *The Epistle to the Romans*, p. 540.

11. Mounce, *Romans*, p. 278.

12. Barton, Veerman, and Wilson, *Romans*, p. 294.

to those in its grasp. Rather, like Jesus, he wants us to be "shrewd as serpents and innocent as doves" (Matt. 10:16).

⊙ ⊙ Living Insights

"You interpret the verse the way you want, and I'll interpret it the way I want."

Have you ever heard someone say this? Then you know that it usually comes at the end of a long discussion in which you and the person with whom you're speaking realize that you are not going to agree. So he or she tries to end the conversation with this "let's agree to disagree" offer.

Unfortunately, we can't accept this proposal. Remember, we're not talking about personal convictions or gray areas in which we must leave room for liberty. We're talking about doctrine and the interpretation of Scripture. To accept such a proposal would be to agree that the Bible had no truth of its own to declare, but its meaning was left up to individuals to decide for themselves.

But God's Word isn't passive like that. It is "living and active and sharper than any two-edged sword" (Heb. 4:12). God's Word accomplishes what *He* desires (Isa. 55:11).

You see, the Scriptures have a unity of purpose, a singleness of aim. To pick and choose convenient meanings of isolated verses is to divorce Scripture from itself—which violates God's intent for His Word to be taken as a whole.

So when we're seeking the meaning of a verse or passage, or if we're testing the meaning of someone else's interpretation, let's remember to:

- see how the passage relates to similar passages

- keep the passage rooted in its scriptural context

- seek to understand the author's original intent for his audience

- make sure the interpretation is consistent with sound doctrine

When we do these things, as well as wait on the Spirit's guidance, we can keep ourselves safe from false teachers and learn how to handle accurately the word of truth (2 Tim. 2:15).

Chapter 15

Unseen Evil and Uplifting Good
Romans 16:19b–24

What words come to mind when you think of Satan?

Prince of Darkness

Father of Lies

MURDERER **ADVERSARY**

The Evil One The Accuser

Devil Blockhead

Wait a minute—"Blockhead"? I've never heard that one before; have you? However, that is how one of the great Puritan preachers described him:

> America's great theologian Jonathan Edwards was right to call Satan the greatest blockhead the world has ever known. For although Satan is exceedingly knowledgeable and cunning, he was also supremely stupid to suppose that he could out-think the all-wise God or overpower the Almighty.[1]

Yes, Satan is a powerful, voracious, vicious enemy; an enemy whose destruction is very real. But he is also a *conquered* enemy whose folly and defeat will be written across the sky when Christ comes in His glory. Until that time, though, how are we to deal with him and the evil he foments? Paul has some sound advice for us in Romans 16:19b–24.

---

1. James Montgomery Boice, *Romans, Volume 4: The New Humanity (Romans 12–16)* (Grand Rapids, Mich.: Baker Books, 1995), p. 1939. Used by permission.

Wisdom and Innocence

We touched on Paul's counsel in our previous chapter, but it is certainly worth a more in-depth look.

> I want you to be wise in what is good and innocent in what is evil. (Rom. 16:19b)

This seems like straightforward advice, doesn't it? Yet in our day good and evil, wisdom and innocence, are often turned on their heads. Let's take some time to straighten out our perspective and understand God's values more deeply.

Be Wise in Good

If we are going to be "wise in what is good," then we first need to understand what "good" is. Certainly, good in this context includes the idea of sound doctrine, such as Paul has been teaching throughout Romans. But it's bigger and more personal than that. A helpful place to start learning what good is all about is Galatians 5:

> The fruit of the Spirit is love, joy, peace, patience, kindness, goodness, faithfulness, gentleness, self-control. (vv. 22–23a)

To these qualities we could add mercy (Matt. 5:7), purity (Matt. 5:8), compassion (Col. 3:12), justness (Mic. 6:8), truth (Eph. 4:25), humility (Eph. 4:2), harmony (1 Pet. 3:8), righteousness (2 Tim. 2:22), obedience to God and His Word (1 John 5:3), and holiness (1 Pet. 1:15–16). To be wise in what is good, then, is not only to discern and follow sound doctrine but also to walk on God's path of life (see 1 Tim. 4:16).

Why? Well, notice what these virtues do. They build up. They support. They encourage. They foster life. They reflect the character and heart of the God who reaches out to us in love and saves.

What they don't do is harm.

Be Innocent in Evil

Evil, on the other hand, promises pleasure and fun and freedom, but its real goal is to wreak destruction. History is strewn with the human wreckage Satan has left in his wake. Broken trust, shattered minds and spirits, violence, deceit, exploitation, shame, heartache, humiliation, loneliness, fear—all kinds of wounding and harm and pain are the legacies of evil. So Paul urges us away from the path of death and toward innocence regarding worthless and injurious things. This means that we are not only to confess and repent of any evil ways in us (Ps. 139:24) but also to rein in our curiosity and not even explore or experiment with evil. We're to discern it and stay away from it.

In a parallel passage to Paul's words in Romans 16:19, Jesus tells us:

"Behold, I send you out as sheep in the midst of wolves. Therefore be wise as serpents and harmless as doves." (Matt. 10:16 NKJV)

As commentator Matthew Henry explains, we are "not to be deceived, and yet . . . not to be deceivers. The wisdom of the serpent becomes Christians, but not the subtlety of the old serpent. . . . A wisely simple man . . . knows not how to do anything against the truth."[2]

Peace and Victory

From evil in general, Paul next moves to evil in particular: its author, Satan. His reign of terror, the apostle assures us, will be over soon.

The God of peace will soon crush Satan under your feet. (Rom. 16:20a)

Does Paul's image of crushing ring any bells with you? It should—it's an allusion to the first glimmer of the gospel, given way back in the Garden of Eden. Adam and Eve, remember, had succumbed to the serpent's seduction and brought God's curse upon humankind. God also cursed the serpent, but in the midst of it, He promised deliverance for the man and woman:

"And I will put enmity
Between you [the serpent] and the woman,
And between your seed and her seed;
He shall bruise you on the head,
And you shall bruise him on the heel." (Gen. 3:15)

Paul knew that Satan's ultimate doom was sealed and that the God of peace—of harmony, unity, and right—would prevail. Notice,

2. Matthew Henry, Commentary on the Whole Bible, one-volume edition (Grand Rapids, Mich.: Zondervan Publishing House, 1961), p. 1800.

though, that where Genesis says God will do the crushing, Paul has Satan crushed under *our* feet. Because Christ's future victory is assured, we can have present victory now. Be careful though. This doesn't mean we're to treat our enemy lightly—he can and will inflict as much damage as he possibly can. But it does mean that we don't need to be intimidated by him. We have God's power and the power of Christ's blood on our side. "Greater is He who is in you," remember, "than he who is in the world" (1 John 4:4).

Grace and Support

What can keep us faithful in doing good and victorious regarding evil? The encouragement of God's grace and the support of friends He has placed in our lives can.

Grace

> The grace of our Lord Jesus be with you.
> (Rom. 16:20b)

Grace clearly was one of Paul's favorite themes. He probably never got over the wonder of it in his own life, that great merciful kindness of God. And he desires nothing more than to bestow it on those for whom Christ died.

Because of grace, God gives us what we don't deserve, what we can never earn, and what we will never be able to repay.

Because of grace, God's favor rests on us without any merit on our part.

Because of grace, God sees His Son in us and is satisfied with our lives.

There's no stringent rule-keeping, no strangling obligations, no condemnation, no guilt. It's all because of God's grace toward us through our Lord Jesus Christ.

And as God's children, we are to be people of grace—loosening the bonds of personal, not biblical, expectations; relieving, not imposing, guilt; bringing mercy, not judgment, to fellow sinners. Grace gives a break to the people life has broken.

Support

After wishing the Roman believers grace, Paul next conveys some caring greetings.

> Timothy my fellow worker greets you, and so do

Lucius and Jason and Sosipater, my kinsmen.
I, Tertius, who write this letter, greet you in
the Lord.
Gaius, host to me and to the whole church,
greets you. Erastus, the city treasurer greets you, and
Quartus, the brother. (Rom. 16:21–23)

It's tempting to just brush by this list of names, but we'd be
missing some precious insights if we did. First of all, we see in these
greetings the care of Christians for one another. All these men were
with Paul in Corinth, and they cared deeply about their fellow
believers in Rome. Next, we'll see even more as we look at each
of these men individually.

Timothy was a frequent companion of Paul's on his journeys
and, as Paul called him, a "kindred spirit" in the faith (Phil. 2:20).
Leon Morris adds that he

> became a trusted and highly valued helper, for he is
> mentioned as being with Paul a number of times in
> Acts and his name crops up in every one of Paul's
> letters except Galatians, Ephesians, and Titus. And,
> of course, he was the recipient of two of them him-
> self. Paul's many references to him show that he was
> very dear to him.[3]

Paul even considered Timothy his "son" in the faith (1 Tim. 1:18;
2 Tim. 1:2). And in his letter to the Philippians, Paul wrote that
Timothy "served with me in the furtherance of the gospel like a child
serving his father" (Phil. 2:22). This "son" certainly shared his
"father's" interests in the church at Rome. And tradition tells us that
this faithful servant gave his life for Christ, dying a martyr's death.[4]

Paul next sends the greetings of Lucius, Jason, and Sosipater.
Some people believe that Lucius is another spelling of Luke, the
beloved physician and writer of the Gospel of Luke and Acts.
However, Paul doesn't ever call him anything but Luke, so it is
unlikely that this would be his companion, chronicler, and Gospel-
writing friend. He might possibly have been Lucius of Cyrene,

3. Leon Morris, The Epistle to the Romans (1988; reprint, Grand Rapids, Mich.: William B.
Eerdmans Publishing Co., 1992), p. 542.

4. Herbert Lockyer, All the Men of the Bible (Grand Rapids, Mich.: Zondervan Publishing
House, 1958), p. 329.

mentioned in Acts 13:1, but we don't know for sure. Jason may have been Paul's host at Thessalonica (Acts 17:1–9), and Sosipater may have been the Sopater (a shortened form of the name) of Berea who accompanied Paul through Macedonia (Acts 20:1–4).

Whoever these men were, we do know that they were at least Paul's "kinsmen"—not his blood relatives but his fellow Jews[5]— sending their goodwill to the believers in Rome.

Tertius, whose name means "third," was probably a Christian slave to whom Paul dictated this letter. Paul gave him the unique privilege of sending his own greetings ("I, Tertius . . ."). Gaius was most likely baptized by Paul (1 Cor. 1:14) and now the host of the church in Corinth, where Paul was staying. Erastus was a bigwig in Corinth, the city's treasurer. And Quartus, whose name means "fourth," was another brother in Christ.

So in this mix we see slave and free, rich and poor, Jew and Gentile—all equal in value in Christ, and all united in Christ in their care for their fellow Christians in Rome. What a beautiful testimony to the good that God's grace can do!

> The grace of our Lord Jesus Christ be with you all. Amen. (Rom. 16:24)

Lessons and Life

As we conclude our thoughts on this passage of Scripture, we find three lessons.

First, *we can never erase evil.* Satan, though a conquered enemy, still lashes out to inflict damage every minute of every day. Remember what Peter said? "Be of sober spirit, be on the alert. Your adversary, the devil, prowls around like a roaring lion, seeking someone to devour" (1 Pet. 5:8). We can't pretend evil isn't real; rather, we need to overcome it with good (Rom. 12:21), bringing Satan's victims to the safety of God's light and love while we still have the opportunity.

Second, *we need not be intimidated by evil.* What is harder to do: kill someone or bring someone back to life? Satan can destroy, but God's power is resurrection power, transforming power. The Lord

---

5. Though the word *kinsmen* can be translated "relatives," Paul "has used [it] before in 9:3; 16:7, 11" to describe "'fellow countrymen.' We cannot insist that the people mentioned were in fact members of Paul's family." Morris, *The Epistle to the Romans,* p. 543.

has crushed Satan and has been pleased to work His power in us (see Eph. 1:18–20). We can't handle evil in our own strength, but we can fight it in God's power.

Third, *we will never experience victory until we personally appropriate grace*. It is only by God's grace that He called us "out of darkness into His marvelous light" (1 Pet. 2:9). It is only by God's grace that good exists, that we can discern it from evil, that we can walk in it. It is only by God's grace that He defeats the enemy of our souls and grants us peace. So it is only by claiming His grace, standing "strong in the grace that is in Christ Jesus" (2 Tim. 2:1), that we can enjoy the victory He has purchased for us.

May the grace and victory of our Lord Jesus Christ be with you always. Amen and Amen!

Living Insights

The best way to become wise in what is good is to be grounded in the source of good: the goodness of God. A. W. Tozer has written an excellent meditation on God's goodness. Find a quiet place, maybe somewhere outdoors in view of God's creation, and let these truths sink deeply into your heart.

> The goodness of God is that which disposes Him to be kind, cordial, benevolent, and full of good will toward men. He is tenderhearted and of quick sympathy, and His unfailing attitude toward all moral beings is open, frank, and friendly. By His nature He is inclined to bestow blessedness and He takes holy pleasure in the happiness of His people. . . .
>
> The goodness of God is the drive behind all the blessings He daily bestows upon us. God created us because He felt good in His heart and He redeemed us for the same reason. . . .
>
> The whole outlook of mankind might be changed if we could all believe that we dwell under a friendly sky and that the God of heaven, though exalted in power and majesty, is eager to be friends with us.[6]

6. A. W. Tozer, *The Knowledge of the Holy* (San Francisco, Calif.: Harper and Row, Publishers, 1961), pp. 82–83.

As you look at the world around you, what evidences of God's goodness do you see?

_____

_____

_____

_____

_____

_____

As you look at your own life, what do you see of God's goodness there?

_____

_____

_____

_____

_____

What can keep you from seeing God's goodness?

_____

_____

_____

_____

_____

Sometimes we need to train our eyes and hearts to see and appreciate the goodness of God. If you're having trouble tasting and seeing that God is good (Ps. 34:8), then spend at least an hour in the Psalms; they are faithful and true teachers. Here are a few to get you started: Psalms 8; 15; 19; 23; 85; 103; 104; 111; 145.

Chapter 16

TO GOD BE THE GLORY FOREVER

Romans 16:25–27

Just as he began his letter focused on what God the Father has done through Jesus the Son, so Paul now ends his letter in the same way. For Christ was Paul's all in all—his life, his love, his goal. His heart could have been summed up in the words of another saint of old:

> Christ be within me, Christ behind me, Christ
> before me,
> Christ beside me, Christ to win me, Christ to
> comfort and restore me,
> Christ beneath me, Christ above me, Christ in quiet,
> Christ in danger,
> Christ in hearts of all that love me, Christ in mouth
> of friend and stranger. . . .
> Praise to the Lord of my salvation, salvation is of
> Christ the Lord.[1]

Let's join our hearts with Paul's one last time in his letter to the Romans. Here we'll find that the Giver of grace (Rom. 1:5, 7) is also the One worthy to be given glory (16:27).

God's Power to Establish

Paul begins his doxology, his paean of praise, by focusing on God's power to establish us.

> Now to Him who is able to establish you. (v. 25a)

God is able—He has the power—to strengthen us and give us stability so that we can stand firm. As John Stott explains,

> *Stērizō* (to establish) is almost a technical term for nurturing new converts and strengthening young churches. . . . So the vision conjured up by the

---

1. "The Breastplate of St. Patrick" (or "I Bind unto Myself Today"), attributed to St. Patrick, paraphrased by Cecil F. Alexander.

doxology's opening words is of God's ability to establish the multi-ethnic church in Rome, of which Paul has been dreaming, and to strengthen its members in truth, holiness and unity.[2]

If we are honest, we must acknowledge that we don't have much stability within ourselves. Everything from Satan to circumstances to hormone levels can shake us up. We're prone to confusion and misunderstanding, and our human limitations and failings prevent us from finding complete stability in one another. No, unifying and settling Christians in community is too big a job for people to do alone—only by God's grace, which He is pleased to give abundantly, can we be established.

And His chief means of accomplishing this is through the gospel.

The Gospel of Christ

Paul wrote that God would establish us

> according to my gospel and the preaching of Jesus Christ, according to the revelation of the mystery which has been kept secret for long ages past, but now is manifested, and by the Scriptures of the prophets, according to the commandment of the eternal God. (vv. 25b–26a)

Because he was "set apart for the gospel of God" (1:1), because God had entrusted His message to Paul, the apostle could call the gospel his own. And his gospel was the message of Jesus Christ—incarnate, crucified, resurrected, and ascended. It was about the One who justifies, sanctifies, and glorifies. The One who saves and unites Jew and Gentile in one faith. The One whose love knows no limits.

Christ was the One to whom all the Old Testament pointed (16:26), though He was seen only dimly in shadows and glimmers. Now, though, the secret of past ages is told and the mystery is revealed. As Leon Morris observes, "The real meaning of the Old Testament has become apparent only through the coming of Christ."[3]

And it is apparent not just to one group of people but to all.

2. John Stott, *Romans: God's Good News for the World* (Downers Grove, Ill.: InterVarsity Press, 1994), p. 403.

3. Leon Morris, *The Epistle to the Romans* (1988; reprint, Grand Rapids, Mich.: William B. Eerdmans Publishing Co., 1992), p. 547.

A Message for All the Nations

The eternal Good News of salvation in Jesus Christ, Paul writes,

has been made known to all the nations, leading to
obedience of faith. (v. 26b)

From age to age, and from all the ends of the earth, God is at
work gathering a people for Himself through faith in Jesus Christ.
And this faith in God's grace ushers in a new life of obedience to
God's righteous standards (chap. 6). Remember what Jesus told us?
"He who has My commandments and keeps them is the one who
loves Me" (John 14:21). Our obedience to God no longer springs
from law but from love, as William Barclay explains.

> Obedience is not founded on submission to an iron
> law, which breaks the man who opposes it; it is an
> obedience founded on faith, on a surrender which
> is the result of love. For Paul the Christian . . . is
> a man who has fallen in love with the God who is
> the lover of the souls of men and whose love stands
> for ever full-displayed in Jesus Christ.[4]

What better way is there than loving, obedient faith to reflect
the wisdom and glory of God and His Son?

God's Wisdom and Glory

Paul concludes his eloquent doxology with these rich phrases:

To the only wise God, through Jesus Christ, be the
glory forever. Amen. (Rom. 16:27)

Only one God is true, only one God exists: the Triune God—
God the Father, Jesus Christ the Son, and the Holy Spirit. All
others are pretenders and idols, whether they're made out of stone,
money, power, or the person we see in the mirror.

This one God is also wiser beyond our meager comprehension,
no matter how educated and studied our minds are. His wisdom is
infinite, before time and after it, above the greatest heights and
beneath the lowest depths. A. W. Tozer strained to adequately

---

4. William Barclay, *The Letter to the Romans*, rev. ed., The Daily Study Bible Series (Philadelphia, Pa.: Westminster Press, 1975), p. 222.

define God's wisdom with the inadequacies of human words.

When Christian theology declares that God is wise, it means vastly more than it says or can say, for it tries to make a comparatively weak word bear an incomprehensible plenitude of meaning that threatens to tear it apart and crush it under the sheer weight of the idea. . . . It is nothing less than infinitude that theology is here laboring to express. . . .

Wisdom, among other things, is the ability to devise perfect ends and to achieve those ends by the most perfect means. It sees the end from the beginning . . . and is thus able to work toward predestined goals with flawless precision. All God's acts . . . are as pure as they are wise, and as good as they are wise and pure. Not only could His acts not be better done: a better way to do them could not be imagined. An infinitely wise God must work in a manner not to be improved upon by finite creatures. . . .

With the goodness of God to desire our highest welfare, the wisdom of God to plan it, and the power of God to achieve it, what do we lack? Surely we are the most favored of all creatures.[5]

God's highest wisdom and expression of greatest favor toward us, Paul writes, is found in Jesus Christ. In His life, in His death on the cross, in His rising from the dead, in His saving work on our behalf, and in His gathering of people from all races and cultures to be united under Him.[6]

Through Christ, we are reconciled to God. We are able to draw near to the holy, majestic, righteous, and loving God. No wonder Paul wanted to give the glory to God forever! Everett F. Harrison concludes,

The God whose eternal purpose has been described as hidden and then manifested in the gospel of his Son, draws to himself through his Son the praise that will engross the saints through all the ages to

5. A. W. Tozer, *The Knowledge of the Holy* (San Francisco, Calif.: Harper and Row, Publishers, 1961), pp. 59, 60–61, 64.

6. See Stott, *Romans: God's Good News for the World*, p. 405.

come. The silence that for so long held the divine mystery has given way to vocal and unending praise.[7]

To God be the glory forever!

⚬ ⚬ Living Insights

As you reflect on your study of Romans, probably Paul's greatest letter, consider the progression of his thought.

He started the way he usually does, centering his readers in God's grace and peace (Rom. 1:1–17). But then he showed the utter sinfulness of humanity, our utter lostness under the Law (1:18–3:20).

However, God's gift of righteousness through faith in His Son saved us. It is by God's grace that we are justified (3:21–5:21), that we are being sanctified (chap. 6), that we have new strength in our struggle against sin (chap. 7). It is by God's grace that we have His Spirit to guide us, that we are His own children, that we can never be separated from His love (chap. 8). It is by God's grace that we have been chosen as His own and have a marvelous future to look forward to (chaps. 9–11). And it is by God's grace that we have a new and beautiful way to live (chaps. 12–16).

God's grace leads to God's glory, doesn't it (16:25–27)? Follow Paul's example, won't you? Ponder the grandeur of God's grace to you, and then glorify your Lord. There's no better way to end your study of this magnificent letter to the Romans.

7. Everett F. Harrison, "Romans," in The Expositor's Bible Commentary, gen. ed. Frank E. Gaebelein (Grand Rapids, Mich.: Zondervan Publishing House, Regency Reference Library, 1976), vol. 10, p. 171.

BOOKS FOR PROBING FURTHER

L earning to relate to others in love is a lifetime endeavor, full of ups and downs, starts and stops, progress and lost ground. But because God is leading our efforts, we can always be encouraged that He'll make sure we grow. To help nurture your maturity and advance your progress along life's path, we recommend the following resources.

Anderson, J. Kerby, ed. *Living Ethically in the '90s*. Wheaton, Ill.: Scripture Press Publications, Victor Books, 1990.

Boice, James Montgomery. *Two Cities, Two Loves: Christian Responsibility in a Crumbling Culture*. Downers Grove, Ill.: InterVarsity Press, 1996.

Fenton, Horace L., Jr. *When Christians Clash: How to Prevent and Resolve the Pain of Conflict*. Downers Grove, Ill.: InterVarsity Press, 1987.

Foster, Richard J. *Prayer: Finding the Heart's True Home*. San Francisco, Calif.: HarperSanFrancisco, 1992.

Gangel, Kenneth O. *Unwrap Your Spiritual Gifts*. Wheaton, Ill.: Scripture Press Publications, Victor Books, 1983.

Hybels, Bill. *Honest to God? Becoming an Authentic Christian*. Grand Rapids, Mich.: Zondervan Publishing House, 1990.

Mounce, Robert H. *Romans*. Vol. 27. The New American Commentary series. Nashville, Tenn.: Broadman and Holman Publishers, 1995.

Nouwen, Henri J. M. *In the Name of Jesus: Reflections on Christian Leadership*. New York, N.Y.: Crossroad Publishing Co., 1989.

Smalley, Gary, and John Trent. *The Language of Love*. Pomona, Calif.: Focus on the Family Publishing, 1988.

Stedman, Ray C. *Body Life*. 3d ed. Ventura, Calif.: Gospel Light Publications, Regal Books, 1979.

Swindoll, Charles R. *Dropping Your Guard: The Value of Open Relationships*. Dallas, Tex.: Word Publishing, 1983.

Tozer, A. W. *The Knowledge of the Holy*. San Francisco, Calif.: Harper and Row, Publishers, 1961.

Some of these books may be out of print and available only through a library. For those currently available, please contact your local Christian bookstore. Books by Charles R. Swindoll may be obtained through Insight for Living, as well as some books by other authors.

Insight for Living also offers study guides on many books of the Bible, as well as on a variety of issues and Bible characters. For more information, see the ordering instructions that follow and contact the office that serves you.

ORDERING INFORMATION

RELATING TO OTHERS IN LOVE

If you would like to order additional study guides, purchase the cassette series that accompanies this guide, or request our product catalogs, please contact the office that serves you.

United States and International locations:

Insight for Living
Post Office Box 69000
Anaheim, CA 92817-0900

1-800-772-8888, 24 hours a day, 7 days a week
(714) 575-5000, 8:00 A.M. to 4:30 P.M., Pacific time, Monday to Friday

Canada:

Insight for Living Ministries
Post Office Box 2510
Vancouver, BC, Canada V6B 3W7

1-800-663-7639, 24 hours a day, 7 days a week

Australia:

Insight for Living, Inc.
General Post Office Box 2823 EE
Melbourne, VIC 3001, Australia

Toll-free 1800-772-888 or (03) 9877-4277, 8:30 A.M. to 5:00 P.M., Monday to Friday

World Wide Web:

www.insight.org

Study Guide Subscription Program

Study guide subscriptions are available. Please call or write the office nearest you to find out how you can receive our study guides on a regular basis.